No Truth
No Justice

In 1994 Christopher Edwards was found dead in hi
battered beyond recognition by a paranoid schizopl
Christopher—himself also mentally ill—had been i
tragedy occurred despite the fact that information was in the pipeline that his
assailant presented an exceptional risk to other people.

For the next eight years Christopher's parents, Audrey and Paul Edwards,
sought truth and justice at every turn. What they encountered was a wall of
officialdom and red tape: sometimes accompanied by a culture which served to
exclude them at key stages and which was often indifferent to their needs as a
bereaved family and as victims. This ranged from silence to misleading
information, obstruction, insensitive treatment and an attitude of self-
preservation—leading in turn to suspicion and mistrust across the board at the
way public responsibilities were being discharged.

Undeterred, Audrey and Paul Edwards ceaselessly challenged the official
responses and the legal and other processes which had relegated them to the
sidelines. Ultimately, with the assistance of the civil rights organization Liberty,
they sought redress in the European Court of Human Rights where in 2002 it
was established that the UK Government had denied Christopher his right to life
and the criminal justice, mental health and inquiry arrangements were found
wanting at various points.

No Truth, No Justice is Audrey Edwards' personal account of these events from
the day that a police officer knocked on her door with news of her son's death. It
is the story of a ceaseless and arduous campaign imbued with lessons and
warnings about the way individual rights are always at risk of being over-ridden
by the state machine. It describes a David and Goliath struggle in which
decency, openness and proper treatment are placed under scrutiny and some
individuals may have escaped their just deserts. The book also acknowledges the
supreme efforts of certain dedicated individuals to preserve the always fragile
integrity of public services and—on an equally constructive note—makes a
number of recommendations for preventing similar tragedies in future.

In 2002, Audrey Edwards was awarded the inaugural Longford Prize which
recognises outstanding qualities of humanity, courage, persistence and
originality in the field of social or penal policy. The judges 'were impressed by
her success in making the system sit up and take notice, and by her fearlessness
in going against society's current hostility to offenders to embrace ideas of
Restorative Justice, understanding and forgiveness'. As one judge put it, she has
worked to make good out of evil. Audrey is now concentrating on working
through the Essex Restorative Justice Group of which she is Chairwoman and
the Churches Criminal Justice Forum of which she is a member.

No Truth, No Justice

A David and Goliath Story of a Mother's Successful Struggle Against Public Authorities to Secure Justice for Her Son Murdered Whilst in their Care

First published 2002 by

WATERSIDE PRESS LTD

Sherfield Gables
Hook
Hampshire RG27 0JG
United Kingdom

Telephone (+44) (0)1962 855567 UK Low-rate landline calls 0845 2300 733
Fax (+44) (0)1962 855567 UK Low-rate landline fax 0845 2300 733
E-mail enquiries@watersidepress.co.uk
Web-site www.watersidepress.co.uk

Reprinted 2007

ISBN 9781872870 48 9

Cataloguing-in-Publication Data A catalogue record for this book can be obtained from the British Library.

Front cover design © 2002 Waterside Press. From a design for Christopher Edward's headstone by David Crowe commissioned through Memorials by Artists. Back cover photograph of Christopher Edwards taken by Clare Edwards.

Liberty can be contacted at 21 Tabard Street, London SE1 4LA. Telephone 0207 403 3888. Email info@liberty-human-rights.org.uk

North American distributors /Sole agents:
International Specialised Book Services (ISBS)
920 NE 58th Ave, Suite 300, Portland, Oregon, 97213-3786, USA
Tel 1 800 944 6190
Fax 1 503 280 8832
E-mail orders@isbs.com
Web-site www.isbs.com

No Truth
No Justice

A DAVID AND GOLIATH STORY OF A MOTHER'S
SUCCESSFUL STRUGGLE AGAINST PUBLIC
AUTHORITIES TO SECURE JUSTICE FOR HER SON
MURDERED WHILE IN THEIR CARE

Audrey Edwards

With a Foreword by John Wadham, Director of Liberty

WATERSIDE PRESS LTD

Acknowledgements

This book could not have been written without the support of my husband Paul, and I thank him and my daughter Clare for their love and care throughout.

Many of those who helped are identified within the book but I owe particular debts of gratitude to Bryan Gibson of Waterside Press for the decision to publish it and for his advice and to Jane Green for so ably assisting him in the editorial process.

The Reverend Dr. Peter Sedgwick, Assistant Secretary of the Church of England Board of Social Responsibility and Chair of the Churches Criminal Justice Forum has been a constant support over a number of years. I am also grateful to Kathy Piper and Kate McFarlane of the Diocese of Brentwood Justice and Peace Commission for their practical help especially in support of our Restorative justice activities.

Liberty's role is explained in the book but we—and many people in future—owe a huge vote of thanks to that organization for taking on what seemed to be a lost cause.

I have been greatly encouraged throughout by the hundreds of messages of support from members of the community both locally and nationally.

Finally, I must thank the local media—TV, radio and print—which have followed the case from the beginning and reported on every aspect. They have been a great source of encouragement to us and have also done the community a great service for which they deserve many thanks.

Audrey Edwards
June 2002

For Christopher

Not so the innocent; though he should die before his time rest shall be his . . .
With him early achievement counted for long apprenticeship; so well the Lord
loved him from a corrupt world He would grant him swift release.

Book of Wisdom, iv 7, 13 and 14

Foreword

Liberty was privileged to be able to help Audrey and Paul Edwards to uncover a little more about the tragic death of their son Christopher. It is no surprise that the right to life is the first of the rights in the European Convention On Human Rights because this right is fundamental and, as we know from this case, once it has been violated nothing can make up for its loss. Unfortunately the story set out so well in this book is not unusual. Mistakes with tragic consequences all too often lead to failures to admit fault and a tendency to be defensive and to avoid being open.

The death of a loved one is tragic but to have to fight to find out the truth which happens in many cases where the authorities are responsible is not acceptable. To have to struggle for every scrap of information and to be presented by structures such as the police complaints system and the inquests which do not work is an insult to relatives and needs to be changed and changed now. The decision in this case not to have a proper inquiry and not to have one that would involve Mr and Mrs Edwards is bizarre, shocking but unfortunately not uncommon.

Rarely do people have the skills and tenacity to fight on through this mess to get at the truth. It can't be right that people have to pursue applications all the way to the European Court of Human Rights in Strasbourg to achieve some kind of remedy for injustice. Mr and Mrs Edwards had what it takes and this book demonstrates how difficult it is for people to achieve change. We should not expect them to have to do this. The system should work and the relatives of those who die in custody are entitled to expect an open system, one that gets at the truth and allows them to get on with their lives and to deal with their loss.

Audrey and Paul must be congratulated for all that they did to try and change that system. They have made a difference and it is now time for change. No one should be forced to go through that process again. This is an excellent account of what is required to change the world. I hope the book also makes a difference to those who read it.

John Wadham

Director, Liberty

June 2002

No Truth, No Justice

CONTENTS

CHAPTER 1

The Knock on the Door

'There is no easy way to say this,' said the policeman, 'but your son has been found dead in his cell.' It was about 5.00 a.m. on Tuesday 29 November 1994, and the policeman had woken us from an uneasy sleep. My husband Paul answered the door and the policeman established who he was before coming in and giving his awful message. Paul repeated it to me after I had stumbled downstairs, donning my dressing-gown as I came.

I had hardly slept at all that night and remember coming out of an uneasy doze to find Paul climbing out of bed and muttering, 'There's someone at the door'. After glancing at the clock and realising the unearthly hour for a caller, I felt very fearful for our son Christopher, but thought perhaps it was a message that my mother-in-law (who was coming up to the age of 100) had been stricken.

The policeman was sitting on the sofa facing me as I entered the room and as I did so Paul turned in his chair and with a haunted face said simply, 'Christopher has been found dead in his cell'. He helped me into a chair and I remember too well the conflicting emotions which engulfed me. Confusion, disbelief and then finally relief—relief that Christopher's terrible suffering had ended—it was finished.

After what to me seemed an eternity I was conscious that the policeman was asking whether there was anyone else we would like informed—yes—our daughter in London and our local vicar and—no—we did not want him to contact a friend or neighbour to come and sit with us. We had each other. The policeman said he could not tell us any more because he did not know any more. He was only the carrier of the message. We could find out more, however, by ringing a detective at Chelmsford police station after 8.00 a.m. and he gave us the number. He was very kind and seemed concerned that we preferred to be on our own but after reassurances he left. We sat together on the sofa stunned and silent.

•　　•　　•

Christopher had been a bright and observant child, though shy and reserved and he often seemed to have some obsession. As a 14-month-old it had been the vacuum cleaner he pushed from room to room—where he went the cleaner had to go also. If I took Christopher upstairs with me, then I had to take the vacuum cleaner. When I mentioned this obsession to his grandmother, I clearly remember, she said, 'They all have their funny little ways.'

By the age of two he had learned all his numbers by demanding to know what the figures were on the garden gates as we passed them on the way to the shops. He could soon count up to 100 and then by using my fingers I taught him addition. and subtraction. By the age of three his fascination with numbers grew into an obsession with mental arithmetic in the form of a game where I had to ask him questions based on the various ages of our family, e.g. how old would I be when grandma was 100! This could go on for hours if I permitted it and eventually I would say enough was enough.

I remember also that at about the age of four he had a favourite pastime of standing on a chair at the kitchen sink, surrounded by all the measuring utensils in the kitchen such as scales, feeding bottle, measuring jug, measuring spoons, pans, etc. He would spend two or three hours measuring water content, pouring water from one utensil into another. It was a wonderful way of keeping him occupied and doubtless helped develop his knowledge of weights, measures and volumes which was later reflected in his mathematical skills. He never seemed to be bored for want of something to do and was always able to invent something for himself.

Geography was another passion and when he was five or six he had pinned up on the whole of one wall of his bedroom a map he had drawn of France, where we often took our holidays at that time pottering around in the car. He followed this up with a map of equal size of a fairy kingdom to accompany a story he was writing. I still have the text of a story of some 18 chapters which he wrote when he was about eleven years old.

Christopher made an excellent start at a primary school in Pinner but then Paul was offered a good position in the public (civil) service in Australia and we took the momentous decision to move to the other side of the world. Soon after we arrived in Canberra, Christopher started school and again demonstrated that he was extremely bright and hard working. He settled well into life in his new country and school and soon had a good circle of friends. He joined the local Australian Rules Junior Football Club and such was his commitment to learning this totally new game that he received, in 1977, the award for the most conscientious attender who tried his hardest, although I do not believe he ever made the first team.

After four years in Canberra Paul was offered the position of Chief Executive of the State Housing Authority of South Australia and we made another move, this time to Adelaide. Adelaide is a charming city and we made many friends there—we still keep in touch with some of them. Christopher seemed to take the move in his stride and settled into the local high school which had a high reputation academically and which we thought would suit him. He continued doing well and I remember one of his teachers remarking, 'If you are lucky you get a child like Christopher coming through your hands once every 20 years.'

Brains and hard work brought him one of the top half-dozen matriculation results in the state of South Australia, followed by an honours degree in Economics with Japanese from Adelaide University. It was the practice of the university at the end of a first year of general studies to select students to be invited to take an honours degree and Christopher was one of the few selected in his year. I remember typing out for him a long, complicated thesis which had to be submitted for that purpose. At the end of his course the university suggested to him that he might like to consider an academic career, which he refused to do.

On reflection, this might have proved more congenial for Christopher but not at the time. In addition to Japanese, he had learned German at school and taught himself Russian and French; at the time of his death he was taking a Spanish language course. He was also a keen and good chess player who had done well in various tournaments, but perhaps his most loved recreation was cycling.

While he had always been reserved and gave priority to his studies he had also been an active member of the Adelaide University Regiment— largely it must be said for the money he earned—and for one year had been secretary of the University Economics Society, where his main function appeared to be organizing a bus tour of the wineries which surround Adelaide! He had also been a member of the University War Games Club which was based on board games similar to those which I understand are used for officer training. During vacations I supplied many lunches to six or seven students who would turn up for a day's intensive play.

On leaving university, Christopher decided to visit Japan to perfect his Japanese and then cross the Soviet Union by train, practising his Russian on the way. While he was in Japan, Chernobyl nuclear power station exploded causing substantial radioactive contamination of the area through which the Trans-Siberian Railway passed, so he decided to remain in Japan. First he worked in a travel agency in Tokyo and then he taught English to the Japanese at the Berlitz School in Nagoya. The financial rewards in the then booming Japanese economy were substantial and with his thrifty living habits he soon saved some money (which was eventually invested in a Victorian two-bedroomed terraced house in Colchester).

Christopher left Japan finally for England in 1988. His objective was to find himself a management trainee job in some large British commercial or industrial concern as he had decided to return permanently to the UK, which we had left when he was ten years old. Unfortunately the state of the British economy was such that employment opportunities for him were not plentiful and a growing lack of self-esteem, the first indication of his developing mental illness, limited his appeal as a job applicant.

Depressed, he returned to Adelaide after some months but not before he had fulfilled a long held ambition of cycling round England and Wales. Before he left England he bought a mountain bike and spent six weeks cycling up the west coast of England, including Wales, then through the Lake District and across country to Northumberland before returning to London via the east coast.

On his way back to Australia, he stopped off in Singapore for a few days and when we met him at Adelaide airport he looked brown and fit. However it soon became evident that he was tense and withdrawn, so we arranged for him to attend a personal development course at a local counselling centre to help him overcome his lack of confidence. We hoped that with the benefits of the course and a supportive home environment he would soon have recovered from what we presumed to be a fit of the blues which many people experience occasionally. He applied for several jobs in Australia and was eventually taken on by a subsidiary of the world-wide Mars organization, producing pet foods in Albury Wodonga.

We were all delighted that he had secured a well paid job in a world class company. When Christopher had been with the company for a short time, one of his senior colleagues was assigned to Japan and he asked Christopher, at the age of 24, to move into his home while he was away and look after his teenage son. During this period we attended a conference in Canberra and from there we took the opportunity of visiting Christopher in Albury Wodonga. His accommodation arrangements proved to be more than satisfactory and Christopher and the young man in question seemed to get along very well, but we were less convinced about Christopher's responsibility for his colleague's company car which was garaged at the home. Christopher had been told not to use it but he believed this was some kind of internal test by the company to see whether he had the initiative to challenge rules and he drove the car as he chose. This behaviour of Christopher's left a niggling worry at the back of my mind and for the first time I began to feel that maybe something was not quite right.

Although Christopher enjoyed the companionship of his colleagues and the social life of a small town like Albury Wodonga, he did not settle to the work and left after ten months. He then gave himself an extended cycling holiday in New Zealand before deciding to return to the UK via a cycling tour of the USA. He finally arrived back in the UK in February 1990.

We had arranged to be in England when he arrived, because I thought Christopher's sense of self-worth still needed bolstering and that he needed support from the family. The initial idea was that I would provide that support in England by establishing a small home and we would commute periodically across the world. In the end, however, because of a growing concern about Christopher's wellbeing and after much soul searching, Paul decided he would resign his position and we would transfer our home back to England. We returned to Australia with heavy hearts and Paul tendered the required four months' notice. I think his decision perplexed many people but we never explained the reason for what must have seemed an inexplicable decision. By the end of 1990 we had established our home in Coggeshall, ten miles from Colchester, where Paul had secured an appointment as chief executive of the local housing association.

Christopher had found himself a few jobs since his return to England but quite different from those he had in mind during his previous stay. The year 1990 had seen him at work in a DIY superstore and then as a dustman in Crawley, which he enjoyed greatly as he soon established a rapport with the other dustmen who accepted him easily into their circle. At the time we returned he was working in a community service job, providing live-in assistance to a young man in Kettering who had become paraplegic following a motorcycle accident. When this appointment came to an end Christopher returned home to us at Coggeshall and we all had a fresh think about his future.

By now Christopher had accepted that a career in industry and commerce was not for him, but he still wished to make use of the intellectual talents he possessed. Early in 1991 he became aware of a new way of becoming a teacher which did not involve a further year at college and which was aimed at attracting into teaching people like himself who had excellent maths. He obtained a position as a trainee teacher in the London Borough of Hillingdon, where he would learn on the job four days a week and attend training college on the fifth day. Christopher felt he would like to become familiar with the area before he started teaching, so in the spring of 1991 he moved into a rented room in Hillingdon prior to taking up his post in the September.

We kept in touch by telephone and he paid us occasional visits. He was clearly undergoing some internal stresses, as was made clear one day when he returned to Coggeshall and told me of a strange experience he had had on the London Underground. As he was sitting on the train, he felt he was bleeding from his chest and that he was losing God's love. By now I was extremely anxious about his state of mind, but although I pressed him to stay he would not do so and he immediately returned to Hillingdon.

Despite our anxieties Christopher seemed to be functioning well enough until one evening we received a phone call from the vicar at Hillingdon, who asked us whether we were aware that Christopher was insisting on immediate confirmation into the Anglican Church and to this end was interrupting church services and persistently visiting the vicarage. The vicar was, of course, pleased to encourage Christopher to join the next confirmation class in the parish, but this was not sufficient for Christopher who felt he needed to be confirmed immediately or he 'would be lost.' No amount of rational explanation would convince his normally very rational mind why this was not appropriate, which was an indication to us that something was going seriously astray in his thinking.

•   •   •

Christopher had been baptised and initially brought up as a Roman Catholic and had made his First Communion in the Catholic church at Pinner in north-west London where we then lived. Like the majority of youngsters he lost interest in organized religion as a teenager. His interest was not rekindled until his first year at Adelaide University and then in a most unfortunate way. He was attracted to a religious group called 'The Navigators', who seemed to have had a strong influence over him. An indication of this was when Christopher told me while I was working in the kitchen that he was an evil person. I was very disturbed at this statement as it would not be possible to find a more gentle, considerate or kinder young man than Christopher and I immediately told him so and asked how he had come to form such an absurd opinion of himself. He then told me that the approach of The Navigators had led him to feel unworthy and indeed even that he was evil.

We naturally tried to persuade him of the absurdity of such an opinion of himself and, as a first step, contacted the Anglican chaplain to the university, who happened to live in the same street as ourselves. He told us that The Navigators, who seemed to aim their approach at the more sensitive and withdrawn students, were active in the university and, in his view, had caused a lot of problems.

One evening shortly afterwards we sat around a table with Christopher, his sister Clare and the chaplain and talked the matter through. As a result Christopher agreed to sever his connection with The Navigators. We encouraged him to maintain his Christian connection through adherence to the Anglican tradition as I was and am a committed Anglican. The Anglican church was only 100 yards or so across the green and we felt that the gentler, more flexible tradition of Anglican Christianity would be a more appropriate counterweight to the stricter approach of The Navigators than the Roman Catholic tradition in which Christopher, following his father, had been baptised.

Christopher became a very devout member of the local Anglican church in Australia: he was an altar server and took communion regularly every Sunday. He was never, however, confirmed and it seemed this was at the root of his demands in Hillingdon for instant confirmation. He had convinced himself that it had been wrong for him to take communion in Adelaide because he was not confirmed. Strictly speaking, this was incorrect because while the Anglican Church requires its members to be confirmed before they become communicants, it is willing to give communion to Christians authorised to receive communion in their own churches—as Christopher was in the Roman Catholic Church. His concern, though expressed as a theological doubt, was not one which could be resolved by an accurate theological explanation. The undermining of his personality as a result of his experience with The Navigators had gone much deeper than we had imagined and required, we believed, psychological or psychiatric attention.

•　　•　　•

After we had been alerted by the vicar of Hillingdon, we went down to see Christopher to try and persuade him to act more rationally. While polite and responsive to our pleas he was no less committed to his course of action. He believed that, although they might nominally protest, the local congregation really wanted and expected him to behave in this way. We continued to urge him to behave more rationally but to no avail.

One evening we received a call from Uxbridge police station where Christopher had been taken following a complaint by the curate at Hillingdon. The experienced vicar who was sensitive to Christopher's needs was away and the curate, no doubt exasperated by Christopher's persistent calls at the vicarage which were unwelcome to neighbours as well, had called in the police who had arrested Christopher. We told the police on the phone that Christopher should be kept in police custody so that he did not cause any more disturbance and could receive proper attention but they released him to appear at the Uxbridge Magistrates' Court the following morning. We arranged to meet him at the courthouse.

He was clearly disturbed but did not question the charge against him. We had a long talk with him and then he went to speak to the court probation officer on his own. We had expected him to plead guilty and be referred for psychiatric reports; indeed we were prepared to stand up in court to support or recommend such an outcome. To our astonishment he pleaded not guilty—possibly as a result of his meeting with the probation officer—and after some discussion the police said they would not proceed with any charge and it was dismissed. The supportive vicar had also been in court and afterwards we all had a cup of tea. I remember him advising Christopher to return home with us. There was no doubt in all our minds that he needed to return to a supportive environment where we could try and secure assistance for him. So we gathered up his belongings and brought him home.

CHAPTER 2

Rescue Attempt

We realised Christopher was likely to continue to seek instant confirmation so we warned the local vicar, Father David Beeton,[1] to expect visits and possible disturbances in church from Christopher. He proved to be extremely tolerant and supportive, despite the many irritations which Christopher caused him, and would give him little tasks to carry out and take him on various visits he had to make.

We had also sought the advice of Fr David as to whether he knew of a Christian psychiatrist and he put us in touch with Dr Bernard Heine who was a regular communicant at St Peters. On one occasion Dr Heine was present at morning service when Christopher stood in the centre isle and behaved bizarrely making a declaration of his faith and need for instant confirmation. Paul immediately rose, put his arm around Christopher and led him outside. After some hesitation I followed. Christopher was very silent and unhappy and it was a dejected trio who made for home.

Dr Heine arranged for us to see Dr Christine Murray, a psychiatrist at a private clinic. She considered Christopher was 'quite unwell' and wanted him to stay in the hospital for further examination. We agreed and Christopher, though reluctant, was initially willing to go along with this. Unfortunately, through the inadvertence of the hospital reception staff, he discovered how much this would cost us and then absolutely refused to stay. During the consultation Dr Murray had written out a prescription for Stelazine which Christopher refused to take. Before we left we recovered the prescription in the hope that we could persuade him to take this medication and on the way home we put the prescription in at our local chemist. That evening after we had collected the tablets, we began the task of persuading Christopher to take them. It took an hour and a half of gentle persuasion and explanation before he would take the tablets and even then he only did so to please us not because he accepted that he needed them.

Christopher had two or three consultations with Dr Murray who eventually recommended that he seek assistance under the NHS because she believed the NHS could offer more support. An interview was arranged with a Dr Wright. Christopher was reluctant to go because he never saw himself as being ill or needing treatment but he was persuaded to attend the appointment with me. Dr Wright interviewed him for about 50 minutes and then saw me for about five minutes as he had a meeting to attend. He told me that Christopher was on the verge of a severe mental illness and should have the support of a psychiatric nurse and that it was

---

[1] Although Anglican priests are usually called Reverend, this was the local usage.

also essential he continued taking the medication, Stelazine, prescribed by Dr Murray. He also stated he would not be seeing Christopher again as he was retiring shortly. At the end of the brief interview, I assured Dr Wright I would make sure Christopher took the Stelazine and that I would contact the psychiatric nurse. Christopher's comment on leaving was that it had been no use—he was fed up with telling his story to different people and then nothing happened. After starting out with a sense of optimism, I left that appointment feeling utterly depressed, feeling that it was futile to see a psychiatrist once and then be referred to yet another.

The next day I tried to arrange an appointment with the psychiatric nurse but was told there would be a 12-week wait and that Christopher would have to visit him to be assessed. This did not match my understanding of the wishes of Dr Wright who had already assessed Christopher and had indicated the need of support from a psychiatric nurse. So I rang Dr Wright's office to see whether they could expedite matters—but without success.

•　　•　　•

Life with Christopher during this period was not easy—for him, for us, or for Fr David. Christopher was internally stressed and needed to be continually encouraged to take his medication. In spite of pleadings and rational arguments against pestering Fr David, he could not be deterred from repeatedly pressing the vicar for confirmation, often going to see him four or five times a day, even on one memorable occasion at 10.30 at night. He appeared to find relief from his stress in various kinds of repetitive activity such as pacing up and down, flexing his fingers, pulling his hair and sometimes he drove Paul mad by continually hitting a ball against the back wall of the house with a repetitive thump, thump. He was, however, always co-operative and never aggressive. We would give him tasks like shopping or painting the garden fence. There were even amusing moments, such as when Fr David and I engaged in negotiation with him to make his representations at the 8.00 a.m. service which had a low attendance and keep his peace at the more popular 10.00 a.m. service. He said he would do this out of consideration for his mum.

The calm and supportive family environment, the medication and the tolerance and support of Fr David and the local community eventually brought about some improvement in Christopher's condition. He was able to secure a low level job in the office of the local authority. He was working there when a letter eventually arrived inviting him to the assessment by the psychiatric nurse. Christopher did not wish to go on principle, still less to interrupt his recently acquired employment; besides which he had already been assessed by Dr Wright who had stated that he needed the support of a psychiatric nurse. We understood that their role was to support the mentally ill in the community not to sit in offices to make assessments already carried out by psychiatrists. Next day I rang the nurse to explain that Christopher was a little more stable and had secured a short-term job. I asked whether we could keep the opportunity of a meeting with him open for the future and this was agreed. Some days later we were astonished to receive a copy of a letter from the nurse to Dr Wright saying he had spoken to me and I had said Christopher was now generally coping well and did not need to see him and he was therefore closing the file.

We were shocked that this could happen but there seemed little point in pursuing it. Looking after Christopher was our priority and was consuming of both time and nervous energy and we had no reserves left for challenging the contents of the letter. This was the last occasion on which the professional mental health services had any contact—or lack of contact—with Christopher.

•   •   •

In November 1991 Christopher was confirmed into the Church of England: among the people confirmed at the same time were teenage sisters whose mother was later to play a key role in Christopher's tragedy but we were not to know that at the time. Although he had previously been absolutely convinced that he only needed confirmation to overcome his internal troubles it did not work out like that, proving that the cause of his problems was not theological but an underlying mental disorder.

We did make further efforts to secure professional help, including visiting Christopher's then GP (later struck from the medical register for other reasons) who suggested Christopher would 'grow out of it'. I attended a local meeting addressed by someone connected to social services to whom I spoke personally after the meeting but no useful advice was forthcoming. I also visited the local branch of a national mental health charity which seemed to be a drop-in centre, but while the helpers offered some comfort they were unable to suggest any avenue of help. Paul visited the local secure mental hospital and tried to obtain advice from the professionals employed there. He had to discuss Christopher's problems through a remote voice entry door system but the best advice offered was that Christopher should go and see his GP. This was doubtless very good advice except that it ignored a well recognised symptom of mental illness sufferers frequently do not recognise their own illness and see no reason to visit their GP—and besides which we had already been to see the GP. The only really practical assistance from the professionals who should have been involved was the periodic renewal, at my request, of the medication, Stelazine. This we now understand was against NHS rules because medication of this type should not have been renewed regularly over four years without the doctor seeing Christopher in person at some stage.

We accepted that in practical terms, apart from the Stelazine, we were Christopher's only support and the main burden of this fell on me as Paul was still going out to work every day. I endeavoured by the provision of personal loving support; a calm home environment; a properly balanced diet; trying to keep him occupied by playing cards or scrabble; and involving him in small tasks such as shopping or walking Cromwell, our basset hound, to ensure as much support as possible. When it was obvious that Christopher was becoming tense and more unhappy I would accompany him on a brisk walk of two or three miles, which did a lot to relieve the tension. It brought home to me the necessity of adequate exercise to alleviate the tension which builds up with mental illness. The whole experience was exhausting both physically and emotionally but slowly Christopher became more stable. He never liked taking the medication and periodically declined to do so but in the end after much persuasion would agree to take it, if only to please me.

Although Christopher rarely spoke of his problems it was obvious that he did suffer terrible inner anguish. He had great endurance but one evening as he paced the floor, something he did quite frequently, his endurance obviously reached the limit. After some minutes, during which we had watched with great anxiety, he suddenly threw himself into my arms on the sofa, shaking and weeping, and was eventually sick. I comforted him as best I could and decided that I would telephone Dr Heine. He agreed he would come and see Christopher and duly arrived about 40 minutes later, around 10.15 p.m. By that time, however, we had calmed Christopher down considerably and while Dr Heine had a talk with Christopher for some 20 minutes or so, the crisis had passed and it would have been difficult for him to assess the problem.

•   •   •

Eventually Christopher began to think about employment again and attempted to renew his teaching apprenticeship in Hillingdon, but found they did not now wish to employ him. After a brief period with Colchester council he moved to employment at the Job Centre in Braintree, again in a low level clerical task for which he was overqualified. While stable most of the time he never appeared happy, conveying by his facial expression and his body language a high degree of inner tension. He resumed his interest in chess, went to the local chess club once a week and played in various weekend tournaments at home and away. He was a good player though not the best in the club and, as we discovered later, was well regarded by his colleagues both as a companion and a player.

When his employment with the Job Centre came to an end, Christopher decided to gain some further qualifications and undertook a business diploma course at the Colchester Institute. This aspiration appeared to indicate a degree of improvement in his sense of self-esteem which we saw as evidence of some recovery in his health. Here too he was well regarded by his classmates who appeared to be mainly young women.

By the spring of 1994, when his business diploma studies were coming to a close, both he and we thought it would be better for him to establish a more independent lifestyle in his own home and to do so in Colchester, ten miles away, where there were greater opportunities for employment and a more active social life. This suggestion had been mooted some time previously by Dr Heine but Christopher did not seem well enough then to take it forward. We now felt more confident that he could cope quite well on his own with our support.

The task of looking for a suitable home which was affordable proved to be most enjoyable. Christopher really got into the swing of things and he and I spent many happy hours looking for houses and discussing their merits or demerits. We would borrow Paul's car and Christopher would plan the route, briefly looking at a map and memorising every street on the route. He could take us to areas hitherto unknown and, without consulting the map again, find the right street straight away.

After much searching, we eventually found a pleasant, two-bedroomed terraced house near the centre of Colchester, which Christopher purchased using his own money saved from his time in Japan and with some help from us. We arranged to have a new central heating system and kitchen installed and after much hard work redecorating the house we were all pleased with the result. But although he seemed happy with his new home he was also sorry to leave us, saying as he left, 'I've been happy living here with you and dad, mam.' At these words I felt pangs of anguish and doubt—were we doing the right thing? We all hoped for a better future for him on his own. Paul's view was that he only needed to meet a young woman who appreciated his good qualities and would be prepared to take the lead in organizing their life together.

We did not lose contact of course—we would talk on the telephone most days; we would meet in Colchester once a week for tea; I would often visit the cinema with him; and Paul occasionally called to have lunch with him at his home. His old room was kept at the ready to ensure he always felt wanted and he returned to us often at weekends, when he would collect his washing which I did for him. The hopes for settled employment were not fulfilled however—he had occasional jobs but the only one that appeared to offer prospects was in Customs and Excise and it lasted only a few days. Christopher said he left because he did not like the smoky atmosphere in the offices but it may have been because the expectations placed on him, though well within his capacities, were above his own estimation of his self-worth. But this was not evident to us at the time. He did, however, commit himself to a Spanish language course.

In October 1994, satisfied that he was firmly established in his new home, we took our first extended holiday for four years and went to Canada for a complete break in the Rocky Mountains. On one Sunday we went to church as usual and found the celebrant and preacher was a prison chaplain. In his sermon he made a striking comparison between the Judaic and Christian attitudes to offenders. Under the Judaic code, he said, when a person offended he was excluded from the circle of the community and the circle closed behind him, whereas under the Christian code he was excluded from society but his place in the circle remained open for him to re-enter. We did not realise then how significant this message would become for us.

•   •   •

Much to our surprise and delight Christopher drove our car to Heathrow to pick us up on our return in mid-October. It was reassuring to be greeted by a warm and smiling son. Driving to the airport he had heard on the radio a report that there had been some collapse of construction work at the airport. Realising immediately that this would cause traffic confusion and delay he had made the split-second decision to park at Hounslow and make the remainder of the journey by underground. This ensured we avoided the massive delays others encountered on their return. Though Christopher's mental stability remained uncertain, his brainpower and his readiness to use it to help others stayed untouched. Clare, his sister, was waiting for us at home and so it was a happy family reunion with no hint of the trauma we would face just a few weeks later.

CHAPTER 3

Prelude to Tragedy

Soon after we returned from Canada Christopher accepted an invitation to spend a week with his sister in Ealing. He cycled the 80 miles there and told us on his return that it had been one of his most enjoyable cycle rides. Clare shared a house with two others and as they all worked Christopher was left to his own devices during the day. They all enjoyed an evening meal and general chat at the end of the day in which Christopher participated, though less enthusiastically than the others. During the course of the week, Clare rang to say that she felt concerned about Christopher as he seemed 'very withdrawn' and 'a bit strange'. She could not describe exactly what it was that made her feel uneasy but said she thought we ought to know. I told her that she should encourage Christopher to come home as soon as possible and she promised to do this. At the end of the week he did not cycle the whole way back but took the train to Kelvedon, the nearest railway station to our home, and cycled from there.

He arrived on Saturday morning in a state of high elation. He had decided, he said, to let out his house in Colchester and move to London where he thought there were greater chances of employment and he could resolve another personal issue. He would not make clear what this was but we guessed it was a wish to establish a relationship with a young woman with a view to marriage. He rang up two estate agents in Colchester and asked them to send details of their property management arrangements so that he could let his house.

We were taken aback by the decisiveness and commitment which he showed and which we had long been hoping to see. It seemed impetuous and not sufficiently planned, but he was 30 years of age and maybe we were behaving like over-protective parents. The positive drive to do something was quite untypical of the Christopher we had known over the last four years. While such initiative was welcome, it also seemed too good to be true. We had reservations about the realism of his new approach but we did not think it right to try and dissuade him. Nonetheless I had a feeling of dread—which was compounded when I observed Christopher sitting on a chair, head down, his body twisted like a corkscrew, looking to all intents and purposes like a rag doll. But apart from this short episode he seemed quite well and I tried to put any anxiety I had to one side.

We agreed to look after the letting of his property and lent him our car so he could go and sort out his house, deciding what to leave and what he would take with him. We expected him back that evening or at the latest early on Sunday. During the course of Sunday morning he rang to say he had not made as much progress as he had hoped so he would not be back for lunch. That was fine, we said, we would have our main meal with him in the evening and he could go to London on the Monday.

There was no sign of him during the afternoon and by 5.00 p.m. we began to get worried. We could get no answer when we rang his home. Had he gone straight to London? We rang Clare but he was not there and she had had no word from him. By now I was frantic and feeling quite sick with worry. We resolved that if we had not heard from him by 7.00 p.m. we would take a taxi to his house to find out why he had not returned.

However at about seven o'clock the phone rang. I answered it and was shocked to find that it was the custody sergeant at Colchester police station, who told me that Christopher had been arrested for causing a breach of the peace early that afternoon. Apparently he had approached a young woman pushing a pram and said, 'What a lovely baby—can I come home with you?' She was understandably distressed by this, ran to her mother's house nearby and called the police. Meanwhile Christopher had moved on and approached a young woman accompanied by some friends who were leaving a football match. They did not appreciate Christopher's interest and there was a confrontation, though no fight. Colchester being a garrison town military police are present and they arrived on the scene and held Christopher until the civil police arrived in answer to the earlier call.

In response to the policeman's questions I advised that Christopher had a history of mental illness and had been prescribed Stelazine. I also learned that a psychiatric social worker had been called in and was at the police station but I was then so overcome by the situation that I passed the phone to Paul. After a brief word with the policeman Paul spoke to the social worker, confirming the details of Christopher's mental history and the prescription of Stelazine. Paul said we would come down to the police station to see Christopher but that we might be delayed as Christopher had borrowed our car. The social worker said he would stay to discuss Christopher's case with us. But getting from a small village with no taxi service to Colchester, ten miles away, on a Sunday evening was not easy. Eventually we managed to hire a taxi from Colchester to come and pick us up and then return there so it took us nearly an hour.

• • •

This was the first occasion I had been inside a police station. I found it inhibiting and I recall that it seemed austere and cold. By the time we arrived the social worker had gone. He was the weekend duty worker and had had to leave to attend another case. We had only a brief word with the policeman on duty and then we were allowed to talk to Christopher.

He was quiet and seemed composed, but we recognised that he was more angry and disturbed than we had ever seen him, though he probably did not seem so to the police, accustomed to violent and aggressive occupants of their cells. He told us that he had hated doing what he had done but had felt compelled to do it. It had been, he said, a cry for help. He asked too how he been cured of pestering vicars—we told him it was because he had taken his tablets and he seemed startled and said, 'Oh'. We stayed with him for about 30 minutes and on leaving assured him of our love and support and that we would be at the court the next morning. I embraced him and murmured my usual goodbye—'Love you, Chris'—he gave his usual reply—'Love you too, Mum'. I looked back as he was escorted to his cell and noticed a slightly disjointed gait. It was a heart-tearing moment. I never saw him alive again.

We did not have a good night; I slept for barely three hours but that did not prevent us being at Colchester Magistrates' Court next day as soon as it opened. Again this was a new experience for us. As we had not had time to appoint a solicitor to represent Christopher we were advised at the court that he would be represented by the duty solicitor. As the duty solicitor had not yet arrived we were invited to sit in the reception area and did so nervously awaiting his arrival. We briefed him on Christopher's background and he went to see him; and to deal with other cases.

After he had been to see Christopher he came back and told us Christopher was totally withdrawn, isolated and he had been 'unable to get through to him.' Christopher had even refused to sign the form authorising the solicitor to act on his behalf, but he would do so anyway. He also told us that Christopher's behaviour in the courtroom cells was bizarre (later we discovered he was not only repeatedly banging on the door but had also stripped off his clothes) and because he was recognised to be severely disturbed his case had been transferred to another courtroom where a more experienced bench of magistrates was sitting. There would, he said, be no question of bail being granted because of Christopher's difficult behaviour. At a later stage we were advised Christopher would be the last person to be dealt with in the morning and that because of that behaviour he would be brought up in handcuffs.

I found this news very upsetting and could not bring myself to go into the courtroom and see Christopher so distressed—and in handcuffs—but Paul went in. There were not many people in attendance and when Christopher was brought up he was not in fact in handcuffs. His case had barely started when he tried to climb out of the dock, so the case was suspended and he was dragged back down the stairs. Paul came back to talk to me waiting on a bench outside the courtroom.

I had sat outside the courtroom feeling that the end of my world had come. How could a loving, law-abiding family find itself in this nightmare? I remember very little except feeling quite ill and that the receptionist came to ask if I would like a glass of water. She was very kind and said if I needed anything just to let her know. At one point there seemed to be a lot of banging coming from the courtroom and it was just about then that a group of young people stopped by the courtroom (I took them to be visiting students). One of them said to someone who had just arrived,

'Hear all that noise? There's a madman in there—he's really mad.' It was a piercing, chilling comment.

Paul returned to the court to ensure he was there when Christopher was brought up—this time handcuffed. While waiting for the magistrates to arrive Christopher said, 'See that woman over there? I want to make love to her,' and also, 'The police are all bullies.' But no-one took any notice of these ramblings. The court proceedings were again brief and were interrupted while the duty solicitor, at the magistrates' request, obtained confirmation from Paul that he could provide full details of Christopher's mental history before leaving the court. Christopher was remanded to Chelmsford Prison for three days for psychiatric assessment and as he was taken down from the dock he called out, 'It's all rubbish!' Those were the last words Paul heard him say and the last time he saw him. Pale and with a haunted look, Christopher appeared isolated and not really registering what was going on around him. A magistrate later gave this account of events:

> Christopher Edwards was brought up from the cells. He was clearly in a highly mentally disordered state. I am not a psychiatrist, and so this is a lay person's view. He was withdrawn and hunched up, staring down at the ground the whole time. He scarcely spoke and when he did it was not audible to us on the bench. He did not appear to be giving any trouble to anybody, and he caused no trouble in the courtroom . . . I am not aware of Christopher doing or saying anything that indicated that he was any danger to anybody but himself.

We then sat down with the duty solicitor while he explained the situation. We were asked again for details of Christopher's mental illness and personal history so it could be recorded on a form 'Remand for Medical Reports' which we assumed at the time would accompany Christopher to prison. We were joined for part of the time by the clerk of the court, who was eating her sandwich lunch as she discussed with the duty solicitor what would happen next.

There was a fair amount of discussion between the two lawyers on the legal implications of the magistrates' decision that Christopher should be sent to Chelmsford Prison on remand for the unusually short period of three days for psychiatric assessment. It was evident from what we were told that all the court officials, as well as the duty solicitor, believed Christopher required psychiatric assessment. From what we understood the court had considered whether it could remand Christopher to hospital but concluded that it had no power to do this. The unusually brief remand period was the best solution they could think of. The duty solicitor said that it was now up to us with the Probation Service to find Christopher a psychiatric bed.

We returned home and Paul immediately rang Colchester probation office but they told him he should talk to the probation officer at the prison, a Mrs Godbolt. Paul did so and had a good 12-minute conversation with her explaining Christopher's history of mental illness. Mrs Godbolt was extremely responsive, positive and very grateful for the information given to her which she said was very helpful. It was clear, she said, that on the basis of what we had told her Christopher's behaviour reflected mental illness rather than criminal intent and she would pass this information on to those who would be handling Christopher when he arrived at the prison. We were told we would not be allowed to visit Christopher in prison that day but we could visit him the next day and were invited to meet with prison healthcare staff at that time to give more information about his mental illness. Because of the nature of this conversation we assumed Christopher would be held in the prison's healthcare centre.

●   ●   ●

That evening we were quiet and subdued. Paul tried to emphasise the positive aspects. His opinion was that in contrast to the Hillingdon experience it had been recognised in court that Christopher was mentally ill and needed a psychiatric assessment, as was made clear by the form 'Remand for Medical Reports' that we had been asked to complete. Mrs Godbolt had also been quite constructive and would have passed on the necessary information to those who mattered in the prison.

Christopher's pestering the vicar at Hillingdon had not been taken seriously but now, Paul said, Christopher had broken one of society's rules which was taken seriously. Although Christopher was clearly mentally ill and in prison, this was the bottom of the pit; the necessary public agencies were now engaged in his case and they would see to it that he received the appropriate remedial treatment.

But I was not wholly convinced. I had an overwhelming sense of foreboding and, as usual, I was right in my basic instincts, whereas Paul had tried to rationalise an acceptable picture from the facts.

I had very little sleep that night and spent much of the time reading downstairs; Paul remained in bed half-dreaming, half-awake. He had the impression that Christopher, oppressed by an attack, was saying to him—'Sorry, Dad, but I can't take any more.' Then as outlined in *Chapter 1* we were awoken at about 5.00 a.m. by every parent's nightmare—the early morning knock on the door.

CHAPTER 4

Official Spin

We sat together, stunned and silent, after the policeman went. Nothing could be said or done to alleviate the traumatic effect on us of that awful message. I do remember going to the cupboard and reaching for the vacuum cleaner with a vague memory of vacuuming the house. I suspect this rather bizarre reaction was an effort to try and bring a sense of normality into an unreal and unendurable situation. For most of the next few hours we sat on the sofa, not really feeling anything but a sort of black nothingness, and waited for our daughter Clare to arrive from London.

We had tried to contact Dr Heine the previous evening for advice on getting Christopher a psychiatric bed, and in response to our message on his answerphone he rang us early in the morning when we had to try and explain the situation. Fr David, to whom we had spoken the night before when he had agreed to visit Christopher in prison, had by now been informed by the police and made the first of a number of visits that day. His sympathy and leading us in prayer was as great a support throughout that day and subsequently as it had been a support to Christopher over the previous four years.

At that time we did not know the details of what had happened. The obvious explanation of what we had been told was that Christopher— mentally disturbed and under the stress of prison—had taken his own life. Yet it contradicted all our understanding of him—even in his mental illness he would have had a moral objection to suicide and he was never a quitter. Yet what other explanation could there be?

At 8.05 a.m. Paul rang the police inspector whose number we had been given; the voice at the end of the phone asked Paul to wait while the inspector was called from the canteen where he was having his breakfast. When he came to the phone he told Paul that Christopher had been found beaten to death in his cell and his cellmate, a person with a history of violence, was being investigated on suspicion of murder. This was a sickening message; not only was Christopher dead, his manner of death had been brutal. Far from providing the framework of support we—or at least Paul—had assumed they would provide for Christopher, prison staff had not placed him in the prison's healthcare centre but had required him to share a cell with someone with a history of violence.

After what seemed an eternity we saw Clare running down the road and I ran out to meet her, crying out that Christopher had been murdered. We fell into each others arms, each trying to console the other, returning to the house to endure the never ending wait—for what? Someone to call and see us to explain how one mentally ill young man had been placed in the same cell as another young man who was known to be violent? We felt this would take a lot of explaining.

• • •

Clare told us she had awoken about 7.00 a.m. with an uneasy feeling and looking out of her bedroom window at the front of the house she noticed a police car had pulled up outside. She ran downstairs with a terrible feeling of dread to meet a WPC who told her that Christopher had been found dead in his cell. The WPC was, of course, not aware of any details and she gave Clare a number to ring. Clare was then told that Christopher had been murdered. She immediately began to throw a few things together to make for home and as she did so the WPC offered to drive her, but one of the other young people who was sharing the house kindly insisted on doing so.

Fortunately Clare was able to remain with us for the next three terrible weeks and proved to be a huge comfort and support, in spite of her own mostly unstated but obvious grief. Though our recollection of those days is that we were totally stunned, looking back we are surprised to find just how quickly we reacted. As we heard nothing from the prison, we wrote to the prison Governor and the Director General of the Prison Service, asking for details of what had happened. We also wrote to the Home Secretary, Michael Howard; our local MP, Tony Newton; and the then HM Chief Inspector of Prisons, His Honour Sir Stephen Tumim. The messages we were sending were that there had been a tragic failure, that we wanted all the facts laid bare and we assumed they did too; it would require moral strength for the institutions to be self-critical; and we requested to be kept fully informed about any investigation which took place.

We now recognise what we have since observed in others, that the instinctive reaction to a major tragedy is to want to know what happened, not for recrimination, but for peace of mind. We also shared the common illusion that all of those involved would have an equal wish for the truth to be told so that everyone could learn from the experience.

Fr David, who had been down to the prison, told us that it was swarming with police and that he could not obtain any information. He had, however, discovered that the mother of Christopher's cellmate was in hospital and his nominated next of kin was a clergyman. Upon hearing this, it made me stop to think of the young man who had killed Christopher, his mother, and the anguish she must be feeling at the news that her son had killed someone. I asked Fr David to convey to her through the clergyman our understanding of her position. I asked myself which was worse—to be the mother of a murdered son or to be the mother of a son who had murdered? I found it a difficult question to answer.

The Coroner's officer, a policeman not involved in the investigation, came to see us and explained the role of the inquest. He told us that

Christopher's cellmate, Richard Linford, had been taken immediately to the high security Rampton Special Hospital and that because there was a murder investigation Christopher's body would be subject to post-mortem, so the release for burial would be delayed. He also wanted us to authorise the release of Christopher's medical records. At that point Paul's anxieties got the better of him and he reacted quite sharply, saying we would authorise their release when the Coroner authorised the release of Christopher's body. The officer was taken aback and I had to calm the situation by explaining, 'My husband is always like that'! We emphasised to the officer that we wanted to get to the truth of everything which had happened and to ensure the agencies involved were held to account where they had failed. He helpfully suggested that if that was our intention we would be well advised to keep records of all meetings, phone calls, etc. We followed this invaluable advice thereafter.

●　　●　　●

The next day we authorised the release of the medical records and in the same letter requested that the police investigation specifically address why the two young men were put in the same cell. The Coroner's officer had also wanted a photograph of Christopher to help in formal identification and we sent the most recent one with the letter. Strange as it may seem, I did not grasp the significance of the request for a photograph at that point; I can only surmise I was so traumatised that I could not or perhaps would not grasp the reality of how brutally Christopher had been attacked. In the end he was identified by his dental records as the police could not identify him from his photograph.

There was some local media coverage but we did not wish to be part of it and did not in fact read the media reports until much later. Moreover as Christopher lived on his own, ten miles away, the media did not establish the connection and get in touch with us at that stage. Paul had to advise the chairman of the housing association where he worked that he would not be able to come to work for some time. The chairman visited us and was most considerate. As he was a lawyer we discussed the possibility of issuing some kind of press statement but decided against it because it might attract media attention to ourselves and we did not feel able to cope with that.

After reference to Christopher's address in one local paper Fr David suggested we remove any items of personal significance or value, as he had known of cases where property had been vandalised following a reported death. We needed Christopher's keys and it was agreed Paul would collect them from the Coroner's officer, when he also had a brief discussion with him. Whether due to that discussion or the belated impact of Christopher's death, on his way back Paul felt compelled to call on his Roman Catholic parish priest Fr Arthur Barrow. Despite Fr. Arthur's sympathetic counsel, on Paul's return he was more distressed than I had ever seen him.

Entering Christopher's home was almost unbearable. Everything was just as he had left it a few days ago; the maps he had been studying were laid out on the sofa, his dishes from lunch neatly washed and stacked on the draining board, the house was neat and tidy. He had little of intrinsic value except his TV, computer chess and one or two other small things, but we retrieved items of sentimental value such as his certificates of academic achievement.

Included among his papers was the documentation for him to make a monthly contribution to support a child in the Third World. He must have been one of the few people on income support ready to commit a portion of his small income to help someone in even greater need. How typical. I remember his grandmother telling me that on one occasion while he had been cycling around the UK he had called and stayed with her for a week or so, and during that time he had hired a car and taken her out every day for a ride in the country, stopping for a pub lunch. It was no mean feat for a young man to cope with a frail old lady—well into her nineties—but Christopher cheerfully did so.

By the end of the week the first replies to our letters were being received. The prison Governor, in charge of everything which happened in the prison where Christopher had been brutally killed, advised that the matter was being investigated by the police and that criminal charges were likely to result. He had no access to any of the police findings but wrote that all would be revealed at any trial which might be held.

We discovered later that he had by then already submitted to his head office a report of what his own investigations had revealed but this was not to be shared with the family of the victim. We wrote again asking for details. The impression we received from our contacts with the representatives of the churches was in marked contrast to the impression we received from the public agencies: the churches were concerned with our welfare whereas the public agencies appeared to be primarily concerned with their own.

On December 6 the Coroner's officer took a 19-page statement from Paul, the longest in his career he said. In addition to recounting Christopher's history, Paul emphasised that we believed it essential the police investigation include consideration of why the two young men were placed in the same cell and the identification of any evidence of negligence by individuals or organizations which played any part in the cause of Christopher's death. As the Coroner's officer was not involved in the investigation he could not answer any of our queries about what happened and asked whether we would like to see the senior officer handling the case. I said I thought that would be a good idea so it was agreed the detective inspector responsible would visit us on December 9—ten days after Christopher's murder. Paul's statement took about seven hours and was a gruelling experience, at the end of which, utterly exhausted, I collapsed in tears. The Coroner's officer, a humane individual, immediately insisted that he himself take on the role of comforter which was a gesture of kindness greatly appreciated at the time.

More replies to our letters were now arriving. In his explanation of the sequence of events Derek Lewis, the then Director General of HM Prison Service, stated that the two men 'were seen by prison staff to strike up a friendship whilst waiting in the reception area' and 'they expressed concern to prison officers that they would be parted after the reception procedures had finished.' He also said that staff 'had no reason to suspect Mr Linford might be of a violent nature'. The same information was conveyed in a further letter from the prison Governor in which he stated 'they struck up a friendship in reception and in their cell,' and also by Mr Lewis in a letter to our MP.

In contrast to the Prison Service, the Essex police did not commit themselves on paper to any explanation as to how the two young men first met. Nothing the police inspector said, however, gave us any grounds to challenge the Prison Service explanation which appeared to us to be inconsistent with Christopher's personality and mental condition.

Christopher's naturally reserved temperament, reinforced by his mental illness, made it difficult for him to form casual friendships even in normal, relaxed circumstances. The suggestion that he did so in the stressful environment of a prison reception area did not seem credible. We pressed the police inspector on the issue at this and subsequent meetings, but he stuck to his guns and repeatedly quoted his own history as a national serviceman and his daughter's experience when arriving at university for the first time as examples of how total strangers when thrown together could form friendships. His examples were fine but his explanation did not fit the Christopher we knew so well.

At our first meeting we also pressed the inspector to investigate the case so he would be able to determine whether there had been criminal negligence within the Prison Service and argued that he should, for example, interview Mrs Godbolt, the prison probation officer, who had acknowledged Christopher's mental illness before he arrived at the prison. He said he would do neither. His position was clearly that he was investigating a murder; he had a prime suspect; and nothing else was relevant. At the time the press was full of reports of a canoeing tragedy on the south coast which demonstrated that a person not present at the scene of a death could be found responsible through negligence and we pressed him to accept the relevance of this case. We argued to and fro but he would not shift his position and neither would we. Next day we wrote to him asking if he would obtain authority from his superiors to widen the terms of reference of his investigation, but we never received a reply.

Another issue raised by the police inspector caused us great distress though it was not of his doing. While much of the investigative work was now complete, Richard Linford was not yet fit to be interviewed and his lawyers had indicated their intention to ask for a second post-mortem, to which they were entitled. This would further delay the release of Christopher's body for burial. I remember feeling angry and upset that there was to be yet another post-mortem. We did not understand why: it was known how Christopher had died and I could not accept that it was necessary for a second invasive procedure to take place. We were not consulted or advised—just told it was going to happen. The thought of Christopher's body being put through a second post-mortem was very painful; he had suffered greatly and I just wanted him to have peace.

CHAPTER 5

Reaching for Help

We decided to seek a meeting with our MP, Tony Newton, to try and press for a proper investigation into what had happened. Mr Newton lives in the same village and on Christmas Eve we walked round to his house and knocked on his door. He himself answered and when he discovered who we were he invited us in. On hearing of our experiences, he was sympathetic and he undertook to take our concerns forward.

Although it was nearly a month since Christopher's death, we had still not informed members of our families as we did not want to cast a shadow over their Christmas celebrations. We did tell them very early in the new year and much appreciated the support they offered. Paul's brother David, who lived nearest, had been aware of the newspaper reports but had not associated them with us—no-one expects these things to happen in their own families! We also received sympathetic support from the representative of the charity Victim Support who visited us and was very helpful. We appreciated the kindness she showed, but the support we most needed was not a shoulder to cry on but the truth from the agencies about what had happened—and we did not feel this was being offered to us.

The trauma of those early days was quite horrific and I kept imagining Christopher would walk through the door and say, 'Hello Mum, I'm home!' I remember clearly that one morning I stood at the bottom of the stairs calling for Christopher to come for his coffee. I kept calling and shouting, 'Why don't you come, Christopher?' At the moment of realising the futility of my actions I felt a wave of fear—was I going mad?

Eventually we were told that Richard Linford's lawyers had exercised their right to a second post-mortem which had been completed and, therefore, Christopher's body could be released for burial, three and a half months after his death. We arranged for the funeral service to take place at the local Anglican church Christopher had attended and for his burial in the adjacent churchyard. Although we had been distressed by the delay in the release of his body, in hindsight it proved helpful as we had sufficient time to plan the service with care. The hymns and readings reflected the Christian belief that we and Christopher shared. Our God was a God of Love to whom we should entrust our lives; He was present even in moments of pain and tragedy though we might not understand how; and each one of us had a unique role to perform in life so that even apparent failure was never wasted.

A unique feature of the funeral was the placing of Christopher's bicycle at the front of the church, sensitively covered with flowers representing Christopher, his qualities and his achievements. As Fr David had been close to Christopher and knew him well this was his way of paying Christopher his own personal tribute. Both Fr David and the Roman Catholic parish priest, Fr Arthur Barrow, participated in the service, which was attended by a large number of local people as well as family members and longstanding friends. It was an uplifting and moving service from which we drew great strength and we both wished it would never end. Christopher's sister Clare spoke movingly and we knew just how much courage it took for her to do so.

Immediately following Christopher's funeral Fr David had suggested we contact an organization called Memorials by Artists about a headstone for Christopher's grave. We did so and found the principal person involved was a woman whose daughter had committed suicide. She had wanted to erect a suitable memorial but found this virtually impossible through the normal commercial channels. She had therefore established Memorials by Artists as an agency through which bereaved families could commission specially designed headstones for their loved ones.

She put us in touch with a young stonemason living in Cambridge. We knew what we wanted and eventually after working through a few options he produced a fine artistic realisation of our original concept. On one side of the headstone is Christopher's name with the dates of his birth and death: on the other Christopher on his bicycle is riding into the future with the sun rising at dawn and a dove, representing the Holy Spirit, poised above his head. There is no break at the horizon on the road between this life and the next. Inscribed on the stone is a verse by the Bengali writer Rabindranath Tagore which we had found on a card within Christopher's Bible—'Death is not extinguishing the light. It is putting out the lamp because the dawn has come.'

The funds to meet the cost of the memorial came from an award we received from the Criminal Injuries Compensation Authority. While we appreciated the award it emphasised what was to us a fundamental flaw in the whole legal system in that there is no recognition of the real value of life itself. If Christopher had lived and suffered blurred vision as a result of the attack he would have been entitled to £7,500; for loss of an eye £25,000; for loss of both legs £100,000. For loss of his life the award we received was £4,550. The criminal compensation system appears to rest on the principle that if a person is injured he or she is entitled to compensation with the amount of the award related to the impact of the injury on the capacity to work but in the case of death the award is related to the cost of the funeral and associated expenses. The Islamic system which recognises that death causes a severe injury to the bereaved family because of the very loss of life itself (and involves the family in determining the punishment) seems to us to have much to commend it.

We realised that we would have to be extremely positive and disciplined in endeavouring to establish the truth. We were already beginning to generate a substantial amount of correspondence and notes of meetings etc., so we realised we would need to have some sort of mechanical help as handwriting everything from telephone conversations to reports of meetings was time consuming and tiring. We noticed an advertisement in a local office window offering a word-processor for sale. I enquired and was given a demonstration on what must have been one of the prototypes—an enormous thing dating from the early 1980s. However the price was reasonable and we decided to buy it.

I did not realise then the headaches ahead. Having browsed through the two instruction books which at first reading were not very comprehensible to a non-mechanically minded person like myself, I put off the task of trying to master the monster and for two weeks kept looking at it sitting on the table. However the day arrived when I could not delay matters any longer and reluctantly I started to unravel the wonders of modern technology. After much toil, I managed some sort of mastery of it and the old machine served us well until we managed to acquire a modern computer.

• • •

Early in 1995 we found some valuable allies. We read a newspaper report on the case of Jonathan Newby, another brilliant young graduate who had been working as a volunteer in a home for mentally disturbed people, one of whom had stabbed him to death. The town where his mother lived was mentioned in the article and recourse to the reference section at the public library yielded the phone number of all the Newbys in that town. After some reflection I decided to ring up each number on the list. The first call was in fact Jonathan Newby's mother!

Jane Newby was both understanding and helpful and told us that the most supportive of the organizations with which she had been in contact were the Zito Trust and Sane. A short time after I put the phone down there came a call from someone called Wendy Robinson who in turn had been alerted by Mrs Newby to our tragedy. Wendy's daughter, Georgina, while working as a physiotherapist in a secure hospital, had been killed by an inmate. Wendy recommended that we contact the Zito Trust of which she was a patron and which had been founded by Jayne Zito in memory of her late husband who had been stabbed to death by a paranoid schizophrenic.

We established contact with Jayne and her joint director, Michael Howlett, who had a valuable background of experience and knowledge in mental health and was no less committed to improving the treatment of the mentally ill in a realistic way. Meeting and talking to other people bereaved in similar circumstances was a positive and supportive experience. Having suffered themselves, they knew instinctively how we felt and were committed to identification and publication of the truth of what happened.

One evening Wendy Robinson phoned to say a friend in Maldon had spoken to her about the case not realising Wendy knew us personally. The

Maldon friend had made it clear that people in Maldon knew and feared Richard Linford and had expected him to kill someone, probably his mother whom he had previously attacked. People could not believe that the authorities, who knew him well, had placed him in the same cell as someone else. Later we were to meet more than one member of the community who told us how Richard had long been recognised as disturbed and potentially violent. One mother told us he had recently assaulted her son with whom he had attended school causing her, a local magistrate, to visit the police to enquire what they intended to do about Richard. She was told that Richard's civil rights had to be observed.

We explored every avenue of potential support from public agencies which we assumed were in existence to protect the interests of people like Christopher and ourselves. The Prisons Ombudsman was sympathetic but explained that his powers did not enable him to intervene on behalf of dead prisoners or their bereaved families while the Chief Inspector of Prisons explained that he was not empowered to deal with cases of individual prisoners, even if killed in prison. The Board of Visitors at Chelmsford Prison expressed sympathy but did not think it appropriate to meet with us at that stage to hear of our concerns. There were press reports that the Home Affairs Committee of the House of Commons was meeting to discuss prisoners and while willing to receive details of our concerns, which we were told would be included in the briefing material, the staff made it clear that the committee would not consider individual cases.

We realised there could be voluntary agencies able to help us so we visited the local library and identified the Prison Reform Trust, Inquest, the Howard League and the Prisoners' Advice and Information Line. We wrote the same letter to each, briefly explaining the facts and seeking any advice they could give us. The most helpful response came from the Prison Reform Trust which gave us some practical advice about the need to contact our MP and a lawyer. None of the voluntary agencies was able to help at that time by suggesting a solicitor with experience in this field who could represent us.

We were not having much luck with lawyers either. The Zito Trust had suggested one or two firms of solicitors and I rang up one particularly favoured by Jayne Zito. An appointment was made and they asked us to send details of the facts which we knew and the concerns we had so that they would be briefed for the meeting. We did so but after they had received this information they rang up and explained it was not the particular area of expertise of the lawyer we had contacted and our case was being passed to another member of the firm who would contact us. I rang up the secretary of the lawyer mentioned on two occasions, who promised to ring us back, but we never heard from that firm again. It appeared to us that it might have been because we were not eligible for legal aid. Other legal firms we contacted proved equally unresponsive.

By this time we had become aware of an organization called Prison Watch and one week we attended a meeting in Derby. About half a dozen families were represented, all of whom had lost a family member through a death in custody, all suicides except for Christopher. They had all had similar experiences to ourselves with obstruction and lack of support from the Prison Service. It also emerged that in each case the prison had not returned the victim's money or valuable items of property. In one case a family had been informed by a Governor that a letter of probate would have to be produced before the belongings were released and the family could not afford to do this. All those at the meeting at the outset were white families but during the course of the afternoon a black couple arrived. It seemed to us that they had been led to believe that deaths in custody affected only black families and they were astonished, therefore, to discover that the other families present were all white.

The one exception to this general blank wall of no response was General Sir David Ramsbotham, HM Chief Inspector of Prisons. It had been arranged that Jayne Zito was to attend a meeting with Sir David and she invited us to join her. Unlike other people in high official positions we found he was keen to listen to our concerns and take them into account in his work. We had occasional later contacts with Sir David and were always greatly impressed by his genuine concern for people, his commitment to putting things right and his readiness to speak his mind. We particularly appreciated his telling criticisms of the medical support available for the mentally ill in prison and his views on the desirability of making mental healthcare in prisons part of the NHS.

CHAPTER 6

Stone Wall

The need for some kind of external support was made ever more clear as little information was coming from the public agencies. To our surprise our letter to the Home Secretary was answered by the then East Anglia Area Manager of the Prison Service who assured us that their internal investigations had revealed no serious defects but we could not have copies of these investigative reports. The Director General of the Prison Service wrote again at the beginning of February 1995 but did not add much in substance. While he did not repeat his earlier statement that the two had met and formed a friendly relationship in the prison reception area, which we had found difficult to believe, neither did he withdraw or contradict it. The police inspector did provide some information—even acknowledging that the police had failed to complete the appropriate form advising the prison of Richard Linford's history of violence.

As the post normally arrived after Paul had left for work I opened the mail each morning and one day was shocked to receive a letter from Derek Lewis, the Director General, in which he described Christopher's death as self-inflicted. This was obviously an error but nonetheless extremely upsetting and I immediately rang Paul to tell him of this latest upset, one of many! Paul as usual managed to console me on the phone and I decided for the time being not to take the matter further. On the evening of the same day we had an apology by telephone from Mr Lewis' secretary. A corrected letter arrived together with a personal note from Mr Lewis inviting us to see him if we wished. Early in March 1995 we also received a copy of a letter from Michael Howard QC MP, the fearsome Home Secretary, to our MP containing his personal assurances that the two Prison Service internal investigations did not reveal any serious defects either in Christopher's reception or in reception procedures in general. This letter was later to become the basis of an unlikely alliance between ourselves—ordinary citizens—and Mr Howard after he left office.

We continued to press directly for an inquiry with the NHS and also the Prison Service through Derek Lewis, whom we met early in April 1995. Also present to take notes of the meeting was Neil Johnson, who was the assistant to the East Anglia area manager who had written to us earlier. We discovered that Mr Johnson had been educated at a secondary school in the same street in Newcastle upon Tyne in which Paul had lived most of his early life and this common bond did help the flow of information in later contacts. We repeated our charge that there must have been serious defects for a person with Richard Linford's known history and behaviour to have been put in a cell with anyone. Unless those defects were identified by an independent investigation and attended to the same tragedy could recur. We also requested copies of relevant Prison Service policy documents and the reports of the internal investigations into Christopher's death. He said he would consider our requests for policy documents and a further inquiry but would not release the copies of the internal investigation reports.

Our notes of meetings did not cover everything which happened but although not recorded I have a vivid recollection of Mr Lewis telling us that he could not add anything to what we had already been told. It seemed at the time that we had to accept the written explanation given to us of why the two men were in the same cell—that they had formed a friendly relationship in the prison reception area, had expressed concern to prison officers that they would be parted after the reception procedures had finished, and that the prison had no reason to suspect that Richard might be of a violent nature—all of which we found difficult to believe.

We cast doubt on the quality of the internal investigations pointing out they had not revealed that Christopher's money had not been returned to us. Mr Lewis appeared greatly embarrassed and promised to look into this urgently. We also challenged his assumption that the prison Governor had provided us with support as he should have done. On leaving the building I felt uneasy; I had been totally disarmed by Derek Lewis who came across as a charming and sincere man. As he had not changed his original explanation for Christopher being placed in the same cell as Richard, I felt inclined to accept it—and yet—the feeling of unease persisted. Something was not quite right.

The outcome of our meeting was that Mr Johnson rang the following day to arrange a meeting when he and the Governor could visit our home and return the money. This was the first occasion on which we had met the Governor. He sat in our sitting room, facing us and a photograph of Christopher, and told us that in all his 30-odd years in the Prison Service he had never seen anything like the death of our son. Staff had been traumatised; many had been given counselling and psychiatric help and some were still on sick leave. I am normally the most sympathetic listener but this was too much. He had not mentioned Christopher at all nor accepted any responsibility for Christopher's death in the prison of which he was Governor. I was provoked by this self-absorbed attitude to point out that no-one in the Prison Service had endured a worse trauma than Christopher, or ourselves, who had received no support of any kind—not even a letter of condolence. Mr Johnson then rather sheepishly offered counselling, but I refused as I felt it was rather humiliating to be treated as an afterthought.

The Governor repeated an invitation which Derek Lewis had made for us to visit the prison and see the cell where Christopher had died as apparently it often helps the bereaved to visit the site of a tragedy. Neither of us could accept this invitation at the time; I could not even drive past the prison without feeling sick and panic stricken and had to look away. Paul did visit the prison later in the year when we discovered that they still held Christopher's clothes and steeled himself to enter the cell. It was not the awesome experience he had feared; somehow the frequency of use of the cell by many prisoners since the tragedy had removed any personal connection to Christopher. Paul was, however, able to say a prayer as well as to gain some understanding of the environment in which Christopher had been placed. I still have no wish to visit that cell.

We also went through a formal process of complaint with the NHS about the medical treatment (or lack of it) Christopher had received but this failed to produce any acknowledgement of failure. The NHS responses repeated the Catch 22 of mental illness. Christopher did not believe he was mentally ill and would not seek treatment and the NHS could not be at fault because it could not insist on treatment for an adult who did not ask for it, even though lack of insight into one's own mental health is a characteristic symptom of mental illness. The facts that the NHS knew a private psychiatrist had referred Christopher to the NHS because she thought he was 'quite unwell' and needed the support nominally available through the NHS—and that we his family had been seeking treatment for him—were apparently not relevant.

On one issue the authorities came totally unstuck—in suggesting there was no evidence that we had tried to see a NHS psychiatrist to discuss Christopher's case. Fortunately we had kept the correspondence which proved our point and which we were able to produce. As a result they had to retract and apologise. In dealing with our complaint reliance was placed upon internal documents we were not able to see and, of course, people writing internal documents do not make notes in a way which incriminates themselves.

Further information did come from Essex police although they had not intended to give it. We had a friendly police contact in another part of the country who—under the guise of obtaining helpful advice from his colleagues in Chelmsford—rang up and in the course of discussion obtained the surprising news that Richard Linford had already been charged at Retford Magistrates' Court (near Rampton) and remanded to Chelmsford Crown Court for a later hearing. We were inflamed by this news as we had made it clear that we wished to be informed at each stage of the criminal process—and indeed there was an obligation on the police to keep us informed. We had actually passed by Retford on the day of the court hearing, on our way back from visiting Paul's mother on her 100th birthday, and under any circumstances we would have attended court.

•   •   •

We had been advised at the outset that we should not see Christopher's body because he had been so severely injured. Bizarre as it may seem, because we never had the opportunity of saying our final goodbye to our son, I could never accept the fact that he was dead. There was always the possibility that a terrible mistake had been made—that it was Richard who had been killed and Christopher who was alive, although the knowledge that one's son had killed another human being must be an unendurable burden to bear. If we had been present at the arraignment of Richard, it would have cut short that particular agony by some weeks. It was not until Richard's trial in April, when we saw him in the dock, that we had to accept the reality of Christopher's death.

•   •   •

Before Richard's trial we had our final meeting with the police inspector in our home. It was a tense meeting of which I still have a clear recollection that he was angry that we had obtained information about the arraignment and transfer of proceedings to Chelmsford Crown Court from someone other than himself. He wanted to know from whom we had received the information but we refused to divulge our source and when we asked why he had not told us about the Retford court hearing I recollect he told us straight that he did not want us to be there. We were so astounded by this reply that we did not ask him why.

I was provoked by his attitude and said we understood his position very well but he did not seem to understand ours and that it was vitally important that we were kept fully informed of *all* developments—and that it was his duty to ensure we were so informed. His retort was to question whether we expected him to tell us of every phone call, to which I replied that that would be very nice, thank you. All we wanted was the truth. At that point I recollect that he began pacing up and down on the rug, saying, 'You want the truth do you?' I replied that, yes we did want the truth and waited with a pounding heart while he continued his pacing, hoping against hope to hear some vital new information . . . but . . . only silence. The inspector was obviously under some tension as we escorted him to the front door. As he stepped over the threshold he looked round with a slightly bemused expression on his face and said that every time he left our house he felt he had been in the witness box. We closed the door and ran to the kitchen before bursting out laughing at this remark. It was a much needed release at the end of an extremely stressful meeting.

With our personal lack of confidence in the Essex police growing, we drafted an advertisement to appear in the local media inviting any prisoner or prison officer who could provide information about what happened to come forward. We thought it essential that any information provided went to an independent contact such as a local lawyer rather than ourselves but the lawyer we consulted was not at all keen on the idea so we did not pursue it.

There had been some doubt whether Richard's mental state would permit him to go to trial and as soon as we knew that there would be a trial we arranged to see the Crown prosecutor because we had been told by the police inspector that Richard had claimed Christopher had attacked him. We did not believe this statement and did not want it to be given any credence in court. Richard could not be a credible witness to events at a time when he was mentally disturbed and obviously he had a personal interest in justifying his action. The Crown prosecutor was sympathetic and promised to raise this request with counsel. Our note of the meeting also records that Chelmsford Prison had clearly changed its practice in dealing with prisoners with mental disorder, as many more inmates with psychiatric histories were now being sent to hospital causing problems for defence lawyers who were finding it more difficult to contact them. The Prison Service, it seemed, was belatedly acknowledging in practice the errors it had made but it would not—at that time—acknowledge them to us.

We also had a meeting with the duty solicitor who had represented Christopher, to obtain whatever information we could from him. He gave us a copy of his notes and from the clerk of the court we obtained a copy of the medical form we had filled in. We had no reason to seek these forms other than that we wanted every piece of information about Christopher's tragedy; but they proved later to be valuable evidence. In our note of the meeting with the duty solicitor we recorded that he told us that his contacts—presumably in the legal profession, the police and the Prison Service—had indicated there had been a row between the Essex police and the Prison Service, with each blaming the other for the tragedy.

•   •   •

Before Easter I went to spend some time with Clare in London so I could have a break from the pressure of events. While I was there Tony Newton, our MP, came round and Paul pointed out to him that as a result of reading the independent inquiry report into the death of Georgina Robinson, we had noted that the NHS guidelines[1] laid down that in the event of a homicide by a paranoid schizophrenic the health authority concerned was obliged to undertake an independent inquiry. He commented that this was well spotted and undertook to use it in his representations within Government for further investigation into Christopher's death.

[1] HSG(94)27

CHAPTER 7

The Trial

An inquest is the normal method by which members of a bereaved family find out what happened to the member they have lost—but we learned this would not apply in our case as there would be a criminal trial. Initially we were told there would first be a plea and directions hearing which would be purely formal about the arrangements for the later trial. On the day before this hearing the police inspector advised us it could well turn out that everything would be completed on that day. When we pressed for further information he just repeated what he had already told us. We thought that holding a plea and directions hearing which might turn into the full trial at 2.00 p.m. on the Friday of the Easter holiday week was unlikely to attract much public attention. By now we had become so suspicious of the attitudes of the public agencies that we thought it might even be a deliberate strategy to play down the shortcomings of some, if not all, of those involved. We therefore made sure that the local media, at least, were aware of the likelihood that this could be the full trial.

We arrived early still uncertain as to whether or not we were to hear a trial or a plea and directions hearing and, while Paul went downstairs to meet the police inspector, I waited with Clare outside the courtroom. Another lady accompanied by a young woman and her husband were also waiting. I realised that this must be Richard Linford's mother so, after some reflection, I approached and introduced myself and Clare. Richard's mother was accompanied by her daughter and son-in-law and we embraced each other in mutual understanding and support, both families having been placed in an agonising situation. In different ways each family had lost a son.

Before the formal proceedings started prosecuting counsel sought a meeting with us and it was at this point we were told that these proceedings would in fact be the trial. He advised that Richard Linford would plead guilty to manslaughter by reason of diminished responsibility and this plea would be accepted by the court. Richard would remain in Rampton Special Hospital for an indefinite but lengthy period and any release would be subject to an order by the Home Secretary. He was also at pains to explain that this was not a soft option but would involve severe conditions for Richard. He clearly assumed that our prime objective was that Richard should suffer for what he had done. Our prime objective, however, was to *find out the truth* behind the whole tragedy in the knowledge that only the truth would give us peace of mind.

Victims are often portrayed as seeking vengeance by instituting court proceedings, whereas very often it is the only method by which they can get to the truth; and as we entered the courtroom we were hopeful that the truth would be disclosed.

This was the only occasion we saw the young man who had battered Christopher to death. He appeared wooden and impassive as if he had been heavily sedated. The court proceedings were brief, lasting little more than 35 minutes with only one witness—a psychiatrist who confirmed Richard was severely mentally ill and that there was a secure bed available for him at Rampton.

The story as told by prosecuting counsel was appalling. It was evident Richard was well known to the police and the NHS for his history of mental disorder and violence—which had been demonstrated during the period of his arrest. The Chelmsford magistrates, said counsel, had made it clear that in their view Richard was dangerous. A prison officer had said he should be kept in a single cell and this was done initially but then he had been put in the same cell as Christopher who had also been identified as mentally unstable.

The defence counsel stated that the facts of the case, whereby two people suffering acute mental illness and each needing help in a hospital bed were placed in a prison cell were a scandal. It had been forecast one month previously that Richard could murder someone. Forty-eight hours before the tragedy Richard had been taken to a psychiatrist who had treated him previously, but his diagnosis was that he was not ill but play acting. It was stated during the court hearing that Christopher's left ear was missing and there was blood around Richard's mouth. This news caused the three of us great distress. In his summing up the judge said that he understood the reason why the way the two young men had been placed in the same cell had been described as a scandal but made it clear that his court was not the place to address those issues.

The trial had been an intense experience, particularly the inference that Christopher's ear had been cannibalised. But it had been too brief and too narrow in its focus, concentrating on Richard's mental illness, to be able to give a satisfactory explanation of our concerns. We had no idea of what to expect and felt like spectators who were not involved, yet the trial was about a deep personal tragedy in our family. We had gained some information about what had happened but none as to why or how. More questions had been raised in our mind than had been answered. Nor did it seem a very satisfactory experience from the point of view of the community—there had been no jury, only the one witness, and no-one in the public gallery other than interested family members and the police.

The CPS officer told us that now the trial was over we could ask the police to release copies of the official documentation to us. We had no right to obtain the documents but the police were apparently able to use their discretion and release them if they wished. We resolved to write to the chief constable as soon as possible.

A few local journalists who had attended the hearing wished to speak with us. After a number of interviews, we left the court very shaken and we remember the three of us holding onto each other and trying to find our way back to the car, silent, completely locked into the terrible trauma. After wandering around for a while not really conscious as to where we were going, we eventually found ourselves in the middle of Chelmsford without realising how we had got there. After locating the car we returned home in a depressed state feeling absolutely helpless and alone, not knowing which way to turn to try to search out the truth and obtain some justice for our son.

CHAPTER 8

The Truth

We never lost faith nor our determination to continue our quest to discover the truth. Fortunately a lot of information came to us more quickly than we had anticipated. We had made representations about our need for information and an independent investigation as widely as possible. One morning there was a knock at the door and the postwoman handed me a bulky brown envelope which would not go through the letter box. Inside the envelope we found copies of all the statements taken by the police during their investigation. It was clear, however, that they had not been sent by the police. Reading those statements again and again we discovered what had actually happened. We thought the authorities would almost certainly not wish the statements to be released to us because they revealed, among other things, that contrary to what we had been informed the two young men never met in the prison reception. Such now was our own lack of trust that we immediately took copies and placed them both with lawyers and in a bank safety deposit box, in case the police or other authorities tried to recover them from our house!

The police statements revealed that throughout his attendance at Colchester Magistrates' Court Christopher had behaved bizarrely in the cells there—to such an extent that one of the police officers on duty rang the prison to warn of his disturbed mental state. One senior prison officer was sufficiently concerned that, as he said in his statement, he 'wondered if [Christopher] should be remanded for some sort of mental health report in the prison hospital'. Both he and another senior officer contacted the court to see if it was possible to obtain a warrant which would allow Christopher to go for hospital reports. These requests were rejected, which surprised us in view of our recollection of what had happened in court.

When Christopher was delivered to the prison he continued to behave strangely and was isolated in a holding cell while other prisoners were processed through prison reception. He was then processed on his own and taken to cell D1.6; one of the prison officers taking him there said he was put in a cell alone 'for his own protection'.

During the period of Christopher's arrest a different drama was taking place in nearby Maldon and Chelmsford. Richard Linford, also a graduate, attacked a woman he had known for some time and then her neighbour who came to her assistance. He was arrested on criminal charges and taken to Maldon police station where his behaviour was bizarre. The police were convinced he was seriously mentally ill and called in the police doctor who certified Richard was not fit to be detained. Richard's history of severe mental illness and violence was, in fact, well known to the Essex police one of whom had been at school with him.

The copies of the police statements we had received rev
Richard's childhood had not been easy, for his mother had beer
twice. He had gone to university and, while graduating, had not
as well as hoped, perhaps because of the onset of mental illness. At various
times he had been a patient in psychiatric units where his behaviour had
been such that staff were frightened of him. He had been—or rather was
supposed to have been—under psychiatric care at the time he was arrested
and imprisoned with Christopher.

Five weeks before this fateful weekend there had been a case
conference involving all the professionals engaged in Richard's case. The
minutes record that his GP said he was 'the most frightening patient' she
had ever met and 'he could actually murder someone'; another said 'it is
only a matter of time before he commits a serious injury on somebody'; and
the representative from the psychiatric unit in which he had previously
been resident said the staff 'are fearful' of him—and that 'he goes for the
more vulnerable people'. The meeting agreed that his adherence to
medication must be monitored and that if he failed to take his medication
then sectioning under the Mental Health Act requiring compulsory
treatment in hospital would be considered. We noted that Richard's mother
had been present at this conference, which we thought was right. This was,
however, in stark contrast to our own experience where we received a letter
advising us that the psychiatrist had decided it would not be appropriate to
see us.

Within two weeks of this case conference it was clear Richard was not
taking his medication. However no action was taken even though,
apparently, there was a vacant bed at the Runwell Secure Hospital. The
police inspector present later wrote a memo to a colleague in which he
stated that the impression he got from the meeting was that Richard was
too violent to be admitted to the open mental health facilities in Chelmsford
but they were not prepared to section him so that he could be detained in
secure accommodation. He added that a certain expectation was placed on
him to find a way of having Richard placed in prison as an alternative and
that he was surprised that members of the medical profession felt that this
was practicable or desirable.

Because of their conviction that Richard was severely mentally ill the
Maldon police who arrested him took him to the local psychiatric unit, the
Linden Centre at Chelmsford. The psychiatrist, who knew his case, took
only a brief period to determine that he was not ill but play acting. The
police who were in attendance were so unhappy at this decision that they
asked the psychiatrist to record his decision on the custody form. The
police surgeon now reversed his earlier decision and confirmed Richard
was fit to be detained.

Richard's behaviour in police custody continued to be bizarre: offered a
shower he walked in fully clothed; on the Sunday he asked for a bible and
was given a *Reader's Digest*, the only reading matter in the police station,

and he accepted. He claimed to be a member of the SAS and when he was later taken to hospital again, this time for attention to the injuries he sustained during the criminal assaults for which he had been charged, he refused to co-operate and had to be carried. While in police custody he assaulted a police officer, for which he was charged, and on the Monday morning as he was being prepared for his court appearance his behaviour in the police station was so threatening he had to be struck with a police baton.

Any doubts we had about what had happened were reinforced by finding in the documents sent to us a copy of a letter from the chair of the Chelmsford Prison Board of Visitors (who was also a justice of the peace). She drew attention to advice she had received from a clerk to the Chelmsford magistrates that Richard Linford 'was brought into court by three police officers, this implied that he was considered extremely dangerous by them. Defendants at Chelmsford Magistrates' Court are normally looked after by a gentleman usher or, if considered necessary, by a policeman sent for from the police station. The presence of *three* police officers in court was considered unique and the behaviour of Linford in court was bizarre.' The chair of the Board of Visitors contrasted this situation with a statement by a police sergeant on the radio immediately after the tragedy that Linford was just a normal remand prisoner. She pointed out this was obviously not the case nor had the police been treating him as such during his court appearance.

•   •   •

When the police delivered Richard to the prison they told prison officers of his violent behaviour on the day; they also believed that prison officers remembered Richard from his previous stay, one of them saying to Richard, 'Are you going to be good this time?' The police did not fill in the official form CID2 used to advise the prison formally that the prisoner presented a special risk or had a mental illness (nor had they done that in the case of Christopher). There is no doubt, however, that prison officers recognised that Richard needed special handling for he was not processed through prison reception with the other prisoners from Chelmsford court. Instead he was taken straight to a cell and put in there on his own. As one of the escorting officers (the same one who had placed Christopher on his own 'for his own protection') said, it had been decided Richard 'was not fit to go in with other inmates'. Some time later, however, when two more prisoners arrived this same officer transferred Richard into the same cell as Christopher!

This was the first time these two young men had met; the repeated advice that they had met and formed a friendly relationship in the prison reception was revealed as a total fiction. The Essex police had taken the very statements from which we were now learning the truth and the Prison Service had carried out two internal investigations.

Realising that we had not been told the truth was in some ways worse than knowing what had happened to Christopher. There had been no intention on anyone's part that Christopher should be killed; in our opinion that was the result of sheer negligence and lack of care. But in contrast to errors made under the pressure of the events the information provided to us after the tragedy was given after considered analysis of the facts gathered during official investigations.

* * *

It later became necessary for prison officers to remove Richard temporarily from the cell occupied by Christopher into which Richard had been relocated. This was because Richard's condition on arrival was such that prison officers had decided against processing him with the other prisoners. Richard was, therefore, taken out of the cell (with some obstruction by Christopher) for processing, after which he was returned to Chistopher's cell.

Later that evening they asked for the cell light to be turned off. Soon after midnight the prison officer patrolling the outside of the cell blocks became aware of some disturbance in Cell D1.6 and used his radio to advise the prison officers inside the block. Five prison officers gathered outside the cell and through the door inspection panel saw a bloodstained Richard, standing, and Christopher's legs. The senior officer present recorded later that he thought Christopher had been assaulted, not that he was dead. He did not instruct immediate entry to the cell to rescue Christopher. Instead the prison officers went off to put on riot gear, perhaps because they knew from past experience that Richard could be a very violent and dangerous person. They returned several minutes later and entered the cell—by which time, certainly, Christopher was dead.

CHAPTER 9

Going Public

Now that we knew what the real facts were, we were even more determined that they should be made known to the public via an independent investigation. Only in that way would the truth be made known; the necessary lessons be learned; policies be changed; and individuals and organizations be held to account for their failures towards both young men, their families and the community.

We had much to learn about how to arouse media interest in our case as our first attempts had been quite unsuccessful. Immediately following the trial there was good coverage locally so we had decided to try and bring the tragedy to the attention of the national media. We faxed a press statement together with a copy of a local press report to a range of national media organizations. Our assumption was that each would have a keen journalist assessing all the messages coming in and who would immediately recognise the importance of the issues we were bringing to attention, both by the merits of our statement and the fact that the local media had reported the case. It did not, of course, happen like that and the only coverage was in the *Observer* after an introduction by the Zito Trust.

Jayne Zito had also referred to Christopher's case at a public meeting. Anthony Middleton, a journalist present, expressed a wish to Jayne to follow up the case and we agreed. The result was an extensive and very good article in *The Big Issue* and there could not have been a more appropriate journal. There is a high incidence of mental illness among the homeless who benefit from the sale of *The Big Issue* and they are at risk of imprisonment because of non-conforming public behaviour. We later learned this article encouraged one MP to table some questions on Christopher's case. He too was told by the Prison Service that their investigations into what had happened had produced no evidence that they should make changes to their existing practices.

Jane Newby, whose son's homicide had been taken up by the BBC *Newsnight* programme, spoke about Christopher's case to a *Newsnight* researcher whom she knew quite well and who then rang us up. The researcher seemed a very suitable person to take up the case because she already had contacts in the criminal justice field: she had been involved in the *Newsnight* programme which gave Derek Lewis the opportunity to put his case against his dismissal by Home Secretary Michael Howard.

We discussed the case at some length on the phone; she expressed an interest and then came to see us for further discussion. We heard nothing more at that point but we later contacted her and she came down and went through all the police statements we had received plus other documentation. After reading everything she said she thought the case might not be suitable for her programme but promised she would contact me again in four weeks' time after she returned from holiday. We were disappointed to find she did not do so.

We had quite a different experience with Wendy Holden, a journalist on *The Daily Telegraph*. She wrote an extensive story on the tragic case of Jason Mitchell, a paranoid schizophrenic who, a few miles away in neighbouring Suffolk, had killed his father and two neighbours. Her report prompted us to contact that newspaper to say that Christopher's case was another example of how the public agencies dealing with paranoid schizophrenics were failing in their responsibility to their patients and the community. Wendy came to see us and wrote a full and sensitive report which brought us letters of sympathy and support from around the country as well as alerting policy-makers to the community's concern. The local media continued to show interest and concern and over the next few years maintained this, which we found supportive. Often when we felt depressed at the lack of progress in trying to get the truth known a member of the local media would ring up and ask how things were going. I am sure they did not realise how much their regular contacts were appreciated.

●　　●　　●

We discovered that some groups concerned with mental health were strongly opposed to the way in which the media covered tragedies involving the mentally ill and actively sought to minimise it. While recognising that there were risks that some stories might be presented in such a way as to make readers and viewers think all mentally ill people are dangerous, we still believed it was necessary to encourage public interest in what happens to mentally ill people. If little or nothing is said then those responsible for current practices and policies are not forced to think again and there is no community support for the policy changes and additional resources which are essential. We agreed with those who opposed media coverage that only a small proportion of people who suffer mental illness are violent but we had greater confidence in the capacity of the community to distinguish between the violence of a small minority and the suffering of the great majority. It is only when the public feels secure in the knowledge that the more seriously mentally ill are being properly cared for that it can have any confidence in the Care in the Community policy.

As we became more involved with mental health issues we discovered there were also conflicting attitudes to compulsory medication of those suffering mental illness. In an understandable reaction against past abuses and a dedication to civil rights, many people oppose any extension of it. We knew from experience that Christopher would have been alive and contributing to the community if he had been required to take his medication regularly. We also knew that Richard Linford would have had a more stable, contented and fulfilled life if he had been required to do so also. He would not have killed Christopher nor have been sent to Rampton for an indefinite period, where he is made to take his medication! This refusal to insist on medication at the appropriate time had cost Christopher his right to life and Richard his right to liberty—which seemed to us rather more important rights than the right to refuse medication exercised by someone suffering mental illness of which a characteristic symptom is lack of insight into one's own illness.

It became apparent that there had been for some time strong differences of opinion regarding both publicity and compulsory medication between Mind and others on one side and Sane and the Zito Trust on the other. Marjorie Wallace of Sane, as well as the Zito Trust, were persistently arguing for what we considered the right actions on both issues.

We received a good deal of support from Marjorie and she suggested that, as Christopher's case highlighted many problems in the treatment of the mentally ill, it might be a good idea if she tried to encourage a TV company to make a documentary illustrating the shortcomings of Care in the Community. We agreed but for one reason or another this project did not come about. She also suggested we might be able to help in bringing together the views of carers who approached Sane and wanted to press for change. She arranged for an article to appear in the Sane magazine, inviting those interested to contact Sane—but only three letters were referred to us. We contacted each writer but as they were few and very scattered it was not possible to organize a group. Marjorie was a great support during those difficult days and we much appreciated what she did for us and for others.

At one meeting Marjorie, knowing we had an Australian connection, gave us a copy of a book by an Australian, Anne Deveson, about the difficulties she had encountered with her schizophrenic son who eventually committed suicide. A part of the story described how her concerns for her son made it impossible for her to sustain a new relationship she was forming with an architect. As Paul read it he realised he had met the author and the architect was one of his senior colleagues in the public housing authority. He had not, of course, been aware of any of the sad and stressful story related in the book during the period when he had known the architect and his partner.

One morning we heard John Humphrys on the *Today* radio programme repeatedly pressing a politician with the claim that the problem with mental health services was a lack of resources. We were provoked to write a forceful letter to him with the evidence that Christopher was killed not because of a lack of resources but because of severe shortcomings in the mental health services, the police and the Prison Service. The argument that there was a lack of resources was, we suggested, used as protective cover by agencies whose failings lay in other areas. To his credit John Humphrys responded positively and sensitively and the outcome was a few minutes' coverage of Christopher's case on *Today* a little later on.

There was further coverage of Christopher's case on the BBC after the producer of another radio programme *Face the Facts* (perhaps prompted by the few minutes on *Today*) rang and asked whether we would participate in a programme. At first I said no because I did not want a programme wholly about Christopher to prejudice in any way the proceedings of an inquiry. He rang back later and asked whether we would agree to a broader ranging programme of which Christopher's story was only a part. This time I agreed and the outcome some time later was a half-hour programme which dealt with Christopher's story and our concerns in a sympathetic manner and also presented a factual and hard-headed analysis of the problems arising from so many mentally ill people being sent to prison. Though normally reticent people, we were willing to cooperate with this kind of programme because we were convinced of the need to enlist community support if much needed change was to be implemented.

•　　•　　•

One of the consequences of further public coverage of the case following the trial was the receipt of letters of support from complete strangers. We learned early on that the kindness and sympathy expressed by these strangers was profoundly moving and comforting, while the self-protective correspondence of the public agencies under a veneer of proforma regrets generated in us a cold determination to force them to come clean and acknowledge their failures.

One such letter came from the lady who had been conducting the Spanish language class Christopher had been attending at the time of his death. She told us she had been puzzled and surprised when Christopher had ceased attending and had tried to find out why. Then she saw the press reports with his photograph. She had been devastated when she found out what had happened and remembered him as 'kind, gentle and very clever, but rather hampered by his diffidence and sensitivity.' She ended by saying, 'All the class thought Christopher was a lovely chap.' I later spoke to her on the phone when she recalled that on telling the class what had happened some of the young women had burst into tears—and one student described him as being like an absent minded professor. Christopher had been recognised by all of them as very clever; he had not pushed himself forward—rather the reverse—but he had been very willing to help others in the class and this in turn had helped to bring him out of himself. I shed many tears over this most moving letter but they were positive tears with the realisation that Christopher's goodness had been recognised and appreciated by others. We felt deeply grateful to Christopher's tutor for caring sufficiently to try to find Christopher and for the trouble she took in writing to us.

One Sunday about this time we visited a nearby Greek Orthodox monastery which once a year has an open day. It was a very peaceful occasion and tea was served to visitors at long tables. We were sitting enjoying the tranquil atmosphere when we were joined by three brothers from America whose father had been a Lutheran minister but at some point he and all his family had converted to the Orthodox faith. The young men were all charming and well mannered. One in particular reminded me so much of Christopher that after a few minutes talk I felt a strong irrational desire to take him home, feed him and look after him. Impulsively I said that if they needed accommodation while in the UK they would be very welcome to stay with us and we gave them our address and phone number. By that time I felt I had to make a hasty exit as emotion was welling up. Once in the car despair and an overwhelming longing for my son took over.

•　　•　　•

It had always been the family custom on birthdays and special celebrations that the children would return and we would celebrate with cake and candles at tea time when the birthday girl or boy would receive her or his presents and then we would go out for an evening meal. Our first celebration after Christopher's death was my birthday which proved a very sad occasion. Why do restaurants never have tables for three but only for two or four? On that occasion the agony of looking at the empty fourth chair was unbearable and I had to choke back tears all through the meal. Sadly our family custom of tea and candles and dinner out now seems to have ceased.

CHAPTER 10

The Inquiry

We discovered an unexpected source of support and encouragement when the Essex Coroner invited us to see him. He explained that the prevailing law severely limited the options open to him and that while it was virtually unheard of for an adjourned inquest to be reopened after a trial, he was prepared to do so with the sole purpose of reaching a conclusion that there should be a separate inquiry because other lives were potentially at risk. It was agreed that he would defer further action while we pursued our campaign for an independent inquiry. We were also encouraged by Jayne Zito and Michael Howlett, who wrote independently to the agencies concerned urging such an inquiry. Jayne and Michael were very supportive during a difficult period for us for which we were grateful, and we also knew they were a great source of help to other families who had experienced similar tragedies.

We had another meeting with the Crown Prosecution Service (CPS) to see whether in light of the information disclosed at the trial any action would be taken against the public agencies or any of their employees for criminal negligence. Lynn Officer of the CPS could only suggest we write to the Director of Public Prosecutions which we did—but to no effect. We asked whether the judge would be making any recommendations but this was not the case. She repeated advice she had given at the close of the trial that we could write to the chief constable and ask for disclosure of relevant papers. This we did more than once but the Essex police always had or found a reason why they could not accede to this request. As we had received the documents unofficially we knew their substance, but felt they needed to be given to us officially before we could legitimately confront the agencies with them.

•   •   •

At long last, on 5 May 1995 the North Essex Health Authority wrote and told us, 'It has been the Authority's intention ever since the original incident that a full inquiry should be held as soon as practical.' If this statement were true it is amazing that we had not been notified earlier particularly as we had been making very public representations for such an inquiry. In our judgement, reluctantly driven to do their duty they were putting the best face on it. Now we sought to co-operate with the authorities organizing the inquiry and they agreed to consider our suggested draft terms of reference. In drawing up our proposals we placed emphasis on finding out what had gone wrong in each of the agencies prior to the tragedy and also on how they had performed afterwards.

When official inquiries into tragedies are announced they are usually described as 'public inquiries', which we soon discovered meant only that they were paid for out of taxpayers' funds not necessarily that they were held in public. We had strongly represented that Christopher's inquiry should be held in public but the agencies made it clear this was not their wish. We again wrote to our MP, Tony Newton; Home Secretary Michael Howard; and now to Paul Keating, the Australian Prime Minister (for Christopher had dual Australian and British nationality) asking that government to use its influence for the inquiry to be held in public. We also included the Australian High Commissioner in London among those whose help we sought. We had discovered he was a former South Australian MP and Australian Cabinet Minister with whom Paul had had contacts while chief executive of the state housing authority. He very kindly arranged the submission of a formal note from the Australian Government to the UK Government requesting an open hearing!

The attitude of the agencies did not deter us from writing to Kieran Coonan QC, the nominated chairman, urging that he hold meetings in public. We acknowledged that the public agencies might not welcome the media attention which a public hearing would attract but we believed that a background of media comment would help generate community support for implementation of any recommendations. Nor did we believe the members of the panel would allow their judgement to be influenced by media coverage. In his reply the chairman stated:

> The Panel of Inquiry has held its first meeting today to plan its working approach. We envisage a first phase in which statements will be gathered from relevant factual witnesses. At the end of that phase the panel will identify those witnesses from whom it wishes to hear oral evidence. We look forward to hearing your evidence at that stage. In addition, we will then consider and rule upon the application that you make in your letter. It may also be the case that other interested parties will wish to be heard on the same issue at that time. Until that point is reached we think it premature to make any decision in principle.

We felt reassured that the door to public hearings had at least been kept open but expressed reservations about a former prison Governor, Mike Jenkins, being on the inquiry panel because we had already recognised the strong corporate culture of the Prison Service and were worried that this might inhibit frank and open criticism where this was due. We indicated we would be satisfied if the nominee were endorsed by the then Chief Inspector of Prisons, His Honour Sir Stephen Tumim, but he told us later he was never consulted—though he had no criticism of the person selected. The other members were Robert Bluglass, a professor of forensic psychiatry; Gordon Halliday, a former director of social services; and Owen Kelly, a retired police commissioner.

We had a feeling of euphoria when the inquiry was announced publicly at the end of July. Here was a body of men who had held senior positions in the relevant fields of experience, backed by all of the agencies and with a substantial budget, committed to investigate Christopher's death in all its aspects. Now we felt we could relax: our struggle was over, the authorities had been persuaded to do the right thing and in about a year, the promised completion date of the inquiry, all the details would be revealed in an authoritative manner.

We were told that Angela Roberts, a senior solicitor working for Essex County Council, had been appointed as secretary to the inquiry and that we should establish contact with her. She proved both in correspondence and at a meeting to be helpful and sympathetic and we undertook to forward our representations to the inquiry panel by the scheduled time of end September/early October 1995. We worked hard on the preparation of this document, occasionally rising very early in order to complete it in time, and handed over our 45-page submission when we met her on 5 October 1995. In it we summarised what we knew had happened and identified the questions we would like answered.

It turned out some other important statements had still to be received—in particular none had been received from the Essex police. Ms. Roberts was seeing the panel chairman, Kieran Coonan, the next day and she undertook to raise with him our continuing wish that the inquiry be held in public and that we be given a copy of the transcript of any evidence we gave to it so that we could check the contents. Subsequently she wrote and advised us of Mr Coonan's statement that the position as regards public or private hearings remained as he had previously advised us and that no decision had yet been made on the provision of transcripts. We remained in touch with her about people and documents we thought the panel should see and all seemed to be going well.

We were taken aback, therefore, by a letter we received towards the end of November 1995 from Leonard Gray, a firm of solicitors in Chelmsford, advising us that they had been appointed to act as secretariat to the inquiry. This appointment, it was said, had been made because of continuing concerns expressed about a perception of bias or partiality in a secretariat composed of a team based at Essex County Council. The letter also made it clear that there was still a substantial amount of background work to be done. We were worried that if external pressures could force a change in secretariat, these same or other pressures might force omission or qualification of legitimate criticism in the final report. Moreover we did not see how the public agencies involved could be said to be co-operating fully with the inquiry if there was still so much work to be done—12 months after Christopher's death!

We immediately took up these points in a letter to Leonard Gray and as we had not received a reply a month later we followed up, early in 1996, with a reminder. This produced a response from Mr Coonan himself. The NHS Trust had apparently suggested, and he had agreed, that it would be better to have a secretariat independent of any of the three commissioning agencies and he was also quite satisfied with the co-operation of all the agencies. He also repeated that the decision on whether hearings would be in public or in private would be taken on the basis set out in his earlier letter. We were again reassured. We—and the other parties—would have the opportunity of expressing our views on this issue to the whole inquiry panel before they reached a decision.

About this time there were press reports that the Department of Health was considering changing the guidelines for inquiries because of fears that they led to a culture of blame and induced defensiveness among NHS staff. Notwithstanding our concern over the change of secretariat, we were wholly committed to the value of inquiries. We wrote to both ministers and bureaucrats at the Department of Health and to the media emphasising the importance of these inquiries to the families of victims and urging that victims' concerns be given high priority in any changes.

On 4 February 1996 we wrote to the secretariat asking if they could bring us up to date with the timetable and arrangements for the inquiry. They replied two days later informing us that a directions hearing was to be held on February 19. As we could not afford legal representation we asked Leonard Gray for advice about the procedures. Who would be there? What could we do or not do? etc. We had received no response by the Friday before the Monday hearing, so Paul rang the secretariat and was given over the phone the agenda for the meeting. We prepared notes on each of the agenda items assuming we would be invited as the victim's family to make our views known on each issue.

• • •

Together with Clare, we were accompanied by Fr David Beeton who had known Christopher so well and who continued to be a great support. We arrived in good time and found the meeting room packed with representatives of the agencies involved, accompanied by their solicitors and also in some cases their barristers. I remember feeling downcast and a sense of hopelessness at the thought of just the two of us trying to unearth the truth when so many legal brains were involved for the agencies. I did not have much hope at that time.

We sat nervously in the middle and towards the front of the meeting room, which was a semi-circular, tiered council committee room and awaited the arrival of the inquiry panel whose deliberations on our son's death would be so important to us. To our astonishment only one person appeared who introduced himself as Kieran Coonan, chairman of the inquiry. The other members, he said, were not attending and he also made it clear from the outset that it had been decided all hearings would be held in private. We were shattered; this was not what we understood. Our expectation based on Mr Coonan's previous letters was that we—and others—would have the opportunity of expressing our views to the whole panel before they reached a decision. We had not realistically expected to win agreement to public hearings but we had expected the opportunity to confront the arguments of those who believed in justice behind closed doors. We made our dissatisfaction plain on this and other issues and Mr. Coonan said he would have some good news for us before the end of the hearing.

We waited in anticipation through a lot of legalese about Salmon letters, etc., which was of technical interest to the lawyers present but a side issue for us, but we did not hear any good news. When the hearing was over we approached Mr Randall, the senior lawyer from Leonard Gray, and asked him if he could tell us what the good news was. We said we hoped it would mean that we would be able to sit in on the hearing on certain days. He said he himself had wondered what the chairman had meant by those words. He thought our explanation might be correct but he was unable to offer any definite answer. We immediately followed this conversation up with a formal letter to the secretariat seeking advice on what this good news was, as well as a request for a transcript of the proceedings.

We also raised with the secretariat and with the commissioning agencies the provision of funding for us to obtain legal advice. It was evident from the directions hearing that the chairman was adopting a legalistic approach and that each of the agencies was relying heavily on their solicitors and in some cases their barristers. Employees were able to rely on legal support through their trade union or professional associations. Each agency was to a greater or lesser degree responsible for failures which contributed to Christopher's tragedy but was able to use public funds to purchase legal protection; whereas we, the bereaved family of the innocent victim, had no support if we wanted legal advice. We argued that natural justice demanded we be given funding to pay for legal support for ourselves and our son.

None of the agencies seemed to share our view of natural justice. Our request was turned down and we were left in the situation of contributing through our taxes and council tax to the defence of the agencies responsible for Christopher's death as well as having to bear fully the costs of any lawyers we employed to try and ensure we could put forward our views.

While we were awaiting responses from the secretariat and the agencies on these issues we were invited by Jayne Zito to join her in giving evidence to the inquiry into the homicide of Mary Povey by her mentally ill son, Raymond Sinclair, as witnesses to the effect of these tragedies on families. This inquiry was chaired by Richard Lingham, a former director of social services, and the event was a very informal and relaxed affair—more like a round table discussion than the formal courtroom atmosphere of the directions hearing. The difference between the two inquiries was to become more evident later.

If the euphoria with which we had greeted the announcement of the inquiry was dissipated by our experience at the directions hearing, worse was yet to come. We never received a transcript of the hearing but we were sent the procedural guidelines subsequently issued by the chairman. These did not identify the good news which we had been promised and to our minds dealt wrongly with an issue of great importance to us. From the outset we had urged that the inquiry, whose terms of reference began with the words, 'To investigate the death of Christopher Edwards in Chelmsford Prison', must consider whether the agencies had attempted to cover up their failures and we had been assured this was implicit in the terms of reference. Mr Coonan, however, chose to regard our comments on this issue at the directions hearing as a request to widen the terms of reference. We immediately challenged this both with the secretariat and the agencies, because in our view, which we had made clear at the outset, an inquiry which did not seek to identify whether the agencies had correctly recognised their failings or sought to cover them up was fundamentally and irretrievably flawed.

Despite our differences on these critical issues, we maintained contact with the inquiry secretariat, suggesting people and documents they should see and questions which needed to be answered. The number of matters about which we were not satisfied continued to increase and eventually we agreed to visit the secretariat office in Chelmsford to go through the outstanding issues. We were not regular visitors to Chelmsford and had to seek out the address shown on Leonard Gray's letterhead. As we approached the building Paul became incensed because the main image presented to the world was not of a firm of solicitors but a firm of estate agents! Only my mollifying influence prevented him from turning the car around in outrage that a firm encompassing both a solicitors' practice and an estate agency was responsible for the administration of a critical inquiry.

We did, however, go in to meet Mrs Kent, a solicitor in the firm, and we went through our concerns with her. The following day she wrote, listing the concerns we had raised. These included such matters as the lack of sensitivity in the treatment of ourselves; the failure to communicate with us; the absence of the panel members from the directions hearing; the failure to arrange a full panel discussion about public/private hearings with the interested parties; the very legalistic approach and the denial to us of funding for legal advice; the alleged good news (or lack of it); and of course our strong view that the inquiry must consider how the various agencies investigated their own performance after the tragedy. In addition we had listed half a dozen areas where we requested further information. We had also indicated our wish to comment on the treatment of the family by the various agencies involved, noting that the impact on the family had been a specific area of concern in a recently published inquiry report on another homicide by a paranoid schizophrenic.

Her letter was an accurate and full list of our concerns and she told us that she was sending a copy to the panel chairman prior to a meeting with him later in the week. Easter then intervened but we relaxed in the expectation that now the inquiry had a detailed list of our concerns we would receive a comprehensive explanation.

Although Paul had settled down after his initial reaction at seeing Leonard Gray's office we still remained concerned that the inquiry secretariat operated as an estate agency as well as a firm of solicitors. Its base of operations was Chelmsford which was also the base for Chelmsford Prison, the Essex police and the Essex County Council: these agencies and their staff who lived in the area would be key witnesses before the inquiry. In our view the firm could not avoid the reality that its estate agency business—the main image it presented to the community—might be prejudiced if it acquired the reputation of giving these agencies and their employees a hard time. We thought the difficulties which this situation could create were no less than those which resulted in the Essex County Council being removed from the secretariat role. We wrote to Leonard Gray, the commissioning agencies and the Department of Health urging that an out of town barrister be employed to take the lead role in probing witnesses. This was rejected.

In view of the honest concerns which we had about the dual role of the firm, we were astonished when we were eventually given 'the good news' which the inquiry chairman had promised, namely that the firm of Leonard Gray had been confirmed as the secretariat until the end of the inquiry! This seemed to us a ludicrous attempt to explain an empty promise. In any event we had never previously been told either in the original letter or later that there was any probationary period or time limitation on Leonard Gray's appointment.

We received a further shock when advised of the chairman's response to the concerns we had raised with Mrs Kent and which she had accurately conveyed to him by letter. His response was that he had noted the issues but it was not his intention to write to us on these matters. We were appalled. Paul's initial reaction was to have no further dealings with the inquiry until the issues were resolved. Though equally angry, I was more positive about future co-operation. The issue had come to a head because in the same letter was an invitation to appear before the panel in three weeks time to give our evidence. Our response was to convey our disappointment and anger that our legitimate concerns were being brushed aside. Our confidence in the inquiry was seriously undermined and we could not commit ourselves to a meeting without further thought.

PTER 11

 race to Face

At the outset immediately following Christopher's death we had thought
we needed a solicitor to represent us at the inquest. After some enquiries
we appointed a local firm but we discontinued this arrangement when it
became clear that because there was going to be a trial there would be no
inquest. Subsequently we had contacted a few lawyers, some of whom
made it clear they were not interested. Others advised us that—because
we were not financially dependent on Christopher and not present at his
death—we had no legal or financial claim against any of the agencies, no
matter how grievous their failures might have been. Therefore there was
little, if anything, they could do for us. The legal situation did not reflect
natural justice but we were obliged to accept the position as it was rather
than as we felt it should be. Now, even if we had to bear the cost
ourselves and in the light of experience, we decided to appoint legal
advisers to assist us in our dealings with the inquiry.

Stephen Shaw, director of the Prison Reform Trust,[1] had helpfully sent
us an article by a barrister on a legal ruling which established that HM
Prison Service owes a duty of care to prisoners. Desperately needing some
assistance in dealing with the inquiry we contacted this particular barrister
direct and then on his recommendation a solicitor, Guy Perkins, through
whom we needed to approach the barrister in the prescribed manner. After
an initial meeting with Mr Perkins, in whom we felt we could have
confidence, we then met with both lawyers in The Temple. The barrister
was young, interested in prisons and said he was impressed by the
documentation we sent him. He undertook to put our concerns strongly
before the inquiry panel and would press them to reimburse our costs. We
now felt adequately armed to meet the challenge posed by the inquiry.

We also suddenly realised that the inquiry was relying only on Paul's
initial statement to the police and had not sought a statement from me,
even though I had been more directly involved with Christopher during
his illness (as well as having a mother's intuition). Nor had they taken a
statement from Clare with whom Christopher had spent the last full week
of his life. So Clare and I prepared our own separate statements and
forwarded them to the inquiry.

Mrs Kent rang to finalise the timing of our meeting to give evidence to
the inquiry and subsequently confirmed in a letter that we should attend
for this purpose at 2.45 p.m. on the 16 May 1996. On the day before that
meeting we met with Guy Perkins and our barrister in London, following

---

[1] Stephen Shaw has since been appointed Prisons and Probation Ombudsman.

which Guy Perkins faxed a message in which he confirmed that while, to minimise our costs, he would not attend, we, together with our barrister, would arrive by 2.00 p.m. so that we could avail ourselves of an invitation by the chairman to attend before him—with our barrister—to discuss the questions Mr Perkins had previously raised on our behalf.

These questions covered such matters as what documentation and information would be made available to us; whether we would be able to attend any of the inquiry proceedings; would we be given transcripts of evidence (whether of ourselves or other witnesses); whether we would be invited to make submissions on any issues; and would we first be given the evidence to which those submissions related. We also wished to raise the issues we had brought up with Mrs Kent and about which the chairman had declined to write to us after she had referred them to him.

When we returned home from our meeting with Guy Perkins and the barrister we found the secretariat had left a message on our answerphone that the inquiry chairman would like to see us at 2.00 p.m. the following day. I have a note that records I rang back two or three times but got no response and that eventually the firm's answerphone was connected on which I confirmed we would be able to see Mr Coonan at 2.00 p.m before the hearing at 2.45 p.m. I also noted that I rang again the following morning, May 16, to confirm this arrangement with Mrs Kent.

•   •   •

We arrived at the meeting place at 1.30 p.m. and our barrister at about 1.50 p.m. At 2.00 p.m., Mrs Kent came in and said that Mr Coonan was now ready to see us. I asked her whether Mr Coonan was to see us on his own, and we were told the whole panel would be present. I felt pleased that we would have the opportunity of meeting the panel informally before the hearing, as we had at the Sinclair inquiry chaired by Richard Lingham, and to discuss with the whole panel the issues which concerned us.

We entered the room and found it was arranged formally like a court. The chairman and the inquiry members flanking him on either side sat in a row along one wall. In front there was a space and then a facing range of tables at which the secretariat and other lawyers sat when present. At one side of the intervening space was a table at which witnesses sat and opposite that table, completing the square, were the people concerned with recording and transcribing the proceedings. Each of the panel members and the lawyers had a small screen in front of them on which was displayed a contemporaneous transcript of the proceedings. The situation conveyed a highly formal, structured and restrictive approach, and was quite different to the round table discussion at Richard Lingham's inquiry. The atmosphere at that inquiry had been much more open and informal with no barriers coming between the panel and witnesses. Those proceedings were being recorded and transcribed, but this was being done in another room with only an unobtrusive microphone on the table.

On entering the inquiry room we were seated alone in our designated places; Paul at the witness table and Clare and I in chairs some distance behind the secretariat and the barrister. And then the hammer blow was delivered. The chairman said he intended to deal with the administrative issues we had raised at the end of the meeting but first would go through our statements. This was a complete reversal of the agreed arrangements which I had confirmed with the secretariat over the phone. The intended change had not been mentioned so that we were faced with a totally unexpected scenario.

This change of plan totally ignored our wishes and the importance we placed on meeting with the chairman prior to the hearing to discuss our concerns; nor did it take into account the impact it would have on us bearing in mind attending the inquiry was a stressful experience in itself. If we had been asked to accept this change of plan in advance we would have objected, but we were so taken aback we did not demur. This was principally because we were stunned by the sudden unannounced change of intention; partly because the formalised structure of the arrangements imposed a psychological restraint on any objections; partly because we were separated and not able to consult each other; and partly because the barrister we had asked to represent our interests at the preliminary meeting with Mr Coonan did not object.

Paul was then taken through his statement to the police by our barrister and this was followed by cross-examination by Mr Randall, the senior lawyer from Leonard Gray. My impression was that perhaps because of our expressed reservations about the objectivity of their approach he wanted to demonstrate he could be quite thorough in his questioning. Paul who had many times been through the tough experience of questioning by Australian parliamentary committees was unperturbed by this but it prompted Clare to turn to me and whisper, 'Is Dad on trial here?' I replied, 'I don't *think* so.' At this point I felt so upset that I began to shake and found it difficult to breath. Mr Coonan suggested an adjournment but I indicated to Paul that he should proceed and the questioning continued until the tea interval. I felt that if Mr Coonan was really concerned about my welfare he would not have changed the arrangements for the meeting without advance notice. During the tea break our barrister was called away to a private discussion with Mr Coonan and Mr Randall. After the tea interval first Clare and then I were taken through our statements and subsequent questioning. At the end of this the chairman announced he alone would participate in the administrative discussions. Other panel members would not be involved.

Our barrister then told us that our presence was not required at this stage and suggested we return from Chelmsford to Coggeshall to collect Clare's suitcase and that he would drive Clare into London where she had to return that evening. The meeting was still going on by the time we returned over an hour later, but shortly afterwards our barrister came to report to us. There was really good news, he said. My heart sank—not more good news! He continued that this was going to be a major inquiry and we had the opportunity through him to make a major input on important aspects which would be made known to us at a later stage. We said we were aware that it would be a major inquiry but we would have been more impressed if the chairman had invited us to attend the meeting. The barrister then stated, much to our astonishment, that it was he who had decided to exclude us from the meeting. One of the points we had wished to broach with Mr Coonan was the question of the inquiry meeting our legal expenses in relation to the inquiry and the barrister had promised to raise this matter. When I asked whether he had done so, he hesitated and then said he 'had touched on it'.

Our assessment of the performance of each of the lawyers involved that afternoon, the arbitrary change in the meeting timetable, the negative impression created by some of the questioning, and the deliberate exclusion of ourselves from a key discussion with the chairman wholly undermined our confidence in the day's events. On returning home we prepared a letter to Mr Perkins instructing him to terminate our barrister's appointment.

It appeared the inquiry chairman's view was that our status in the inquiry was as witnesses to certain events in the same way as various police and prison officers were witnesses to other events. Even though it was our son who was the victim of the tragedy we were not regarded as being in any way different from other witnesses. This was a fundamental difference for we—and the agencies had told us they also—believed the family of the victim had a special status by virtue of our loss. It appeared too as if we were regarded by the inquiry as whinging nuisances who should wait for the outcome of the report.

The depth of the impact of this dreadful afternoon is indicated by the delayed reaction of Clare, a very sensible, practical and strong person. Clare told me, later, that next day at the office she suddenly burst into tears for no apparent reason; undoubtedly a reaction to the ordeal of the previous day.

CHAPTER 12

Fighting Back

We had to press hard for a copy of the transcript of our evidence to the inquiry and when we did receive it we noted that there were errors. One error which caused us some distress was where Paul had said Christopher was 30, while the transcript showed 'dirty'. While this error might be understandable we felt it was important to point it out immediately as we did not want a false impression of Christopher to be created. We also wondered whether there might be similar errors in other transcripts which were not made available to the witnesses and which would remain uncorrected.

We were invited to a second meeting with the inquiry panel a few weeks later. Before we attended, the secretariat wrote and asked us to provide the remaining supply of the drug Stelazine found in Christopher's house, which I had mentioned in my evidence, so that Professor Bluglass the psychiatrist could examine it. In their letter the secretariat stated there was no mention of any repeat prescription on the record of Christopher's GP. We forwarded the drugs in their packet, with the pharmacist's label clearly evident, but when we appeared for our second meeting with the panel and the drugs were returned, it did seem to us from Professor Bluglass's reaction that he had not seen them. We are not sure why the request to produce the drugs was made. If the intention was to check that the GP had followed the correct procedure (which apparently had not been done because Christopher had not seen the GP) this should have been raised in their final report but it was not. We wondered whether they thought we had obtained the drugs illegally.

We arrived early for the second hearing with the inquiry panel and passed the time of day with the inquiry receptionist who mentioned that the panel members were being well looked after and that when in session they stayed at the Pontlands Park Hotel. We had never ever heard of this hotel and some weeks later we decided to call in and have a cup of tea. It proved to be a Victorian mansion recently converted to a luxury hotel with a splendid restaurant and a health and leisure centre incorporating a swimming pool. It was set in acres of beautiful grounds with, of course, a price tag to match.

After our experience at the first hearing I pressed that we be allowed to sit together for questioning at the second one and this was agreed. There were some questions about how much the court knew about Christopher's mental illness and here the copies of the duty solicitor's notes and the form 'Remand for Medical Reports' completed at the court which Paul had obtained soon after the tragedy proved invaluable. The duty solicitor had

given evidence to the inquiry but he no longer had his
able to provide more evidence than he had. The m
Christopher's mental health It was a bitter irony: if
professionals had been as interested as the panel
knowledge of Christopher's illness during his lifetim
deemed it inappropriate to see us—the tragedy might nave
The meeting was less intense than before and we discovered during a tea
break that Dr Heine was waiting to be interviewed after us.

• • •

About this time we again asked the commissioning agencies for
financial support to meet our legal expenses. In rejecting our request they
expressed the view that we had pre-judged the process and were
determined to find it wanting. The idea that our criticisms might be well-
founded was not one they could at this stage bring themselves to accept
and no answer was given to the specific points raised other than a rejection
of our request for financial support. At our request, Guy Perkins wrote two
firm but polite letters to the agencies and inquiry secretariat placing on
record our dismay at the treatment we had received. He pointed out that
we were victims of this tragedy and had lost a much loved son when he
was under the care and control of different government agencies and that
we were simply two individuals of limited means who had endeavoured
and would continue to endeavour to find out why it was that our son died.
He also contrasted the treatment we had received with the view expressed
by the inquiry in adjacent Suffolk into the Jason Mitchell tragedy.

> It is our firm view that the families of victims have a most central public
> concern and are key representatives of the wider community whose
> interests inquiries such as ours are established to serve. In our view they
> should be given the opportunity to be present at any inquiry into
> homicides, whether that inquiry be held in public or in private. Such
> opportunity might usefully be provided by the sponsoring authority in the
> terms of reference it gives to the independent panel of inquiry.

In one letter Guy Perkins sought withdrawal of the allegation that we
had prejudged the inquiry and at least this was offered. The first step
forward had been made.

• • •

Jayne Zito had helpfully given us the name of Dr Sheila Adam the
senior bureaucrat at the Department of Health who had responsibility for
these inquiries and we decided to make her aware of our concerns about
the inquiry process. As a result we were invited to meet with a senior
member of staff, Elaine Edgar, to whom we could explain the difficulties

e were encountering. We had mentioned that we had it in mind in due course to write our reflections on our experience. We were now pressed to provide an interim statement which could be taken into account in a review of the inquiry process which was then taking place. We did this and sent it to Elaine Edgar before our meeting.

Our actual experience of relating to the inquiry had, we said, fallen well below our expectations. We felt that the panel and secretariat had a complete lack of empathy with the bereaved family; there appeared to be no strategic plan; and the excessive delay meant the time lapse between the events, the questioning of them and the publication of the report was continually increasing. The inquiry, in our view, had shown itself to be far too sensitive to the wishes of the agencies being investigated by tolerating delays and changing the secretariat under pressure. We felt it was against natural justice to be denied funding for legal support which was readily available to the agencies under examination, and objected to the very legalistic and intimidating hearings of this inquiry compared with the more humane approach we had experienced elsewhere.

We also criticised the refusal to investigate properly the activities of the agencies after the tragedy; the repeated fobbing off with meaningless assurances, e.g. there was good news to come and that the role of the chairman and secretariat was to protect our interests; and we complained of being 'bounced' into the first meeting contrary to arrangements agreed the day before and confirmed on the morning of the hearing. Overall, we said, the impression we had gained was that the inquiry was an exercise by professionals into which the victim's family is not expected to intrude, and that the objective was a damage control exercise for the agencies not a revelation of the truth, however unpalatable. We also made many recommendations based on our experience, designed to ensure the interests of families were properly recognised in the membership, terms of reference and ongoing administration of all future inquiries.

Paul's public service experience was again helpful in enabling us to prepare this submission and Elaine Edgar was clearly concerned at what we had to say. Over a cup of tea she asked questions, thanked us and assured us that serious consideration would be given to all we had said. The immediate outcome of our meeting with her was an invitation to meet representatives of the commissioning agencies so that they too could hear at first hand our concerns about the inquiry—and so that these could be passed on where relevant to the inquiry chairman. We were also beginning to get a better service from the inquiry secretariat, who now provided us with the long-requested list of those who attended the directions hearing six months previously, a schedule of witnesses and a progress report. We were also asked to provide a summary of the key issues of concern to us which in due course we did.

We sent a copy of our reflections paper to the commissioning agencies and it formed the basis of a meeting with them early in October 1996. It was a cordial meeting at which we explained our misgivings and it was followed up by a sympathetic letter in which the agencies acknowledged the distress we had suffered and apologised unreservedly for any part they had played. When I opened and read this letter I was so overwhelmed by the difference in tone from letters so far received that the tears flowed uncontrollably. It was far easier to deal with the usual stonewalling type of letter than one of sympathy which touched a nerve and opened the floodgates!

This was followed up by a more detached letter responding to the individual issues we had raised. This again was couched in sympathetic and constructive terms and concluded with a statement that they were broadly in agreement with many of our recommendations and had already reached several of the conclusions we had.

The meeting and subsequent letters marked a turning point in our relations with the agencies which was all to the good. In part it obviously resulted from the helpful intervention of Elaine Edgar and in part from the rational and fact based nature of our representations. We suspected it might also reflect that the agencies were beginning to encounter some of the same difficulties with the inquiry which we had experienced. They certainly must have been concerned that the timetable and the budget were being over-run.

CHAPTER 13

Encounter of Another Kind

We had agreed with both Elaine Edgar and the commissioning agencies that we were more than willing to meet the inquiry panel to discuss our reflections paper, so we agreed they should have a copy and a date in November was fixed. A couple of weeks before the meeting Mrs Kent rang to discuss the arrangements for the meeting. In my notes of our discussion I recorded her advice that Mr Coonan believed the proceedings should be recorded and that as the equipment was already installed in the inquiry room the meeting should be there, though we would sit on comfortable chairs around a coffee table in front of the bay window. She was very affable and asked whether we would be happy with the arrangements and I said we would agree with Mr Coonan's wishes.

I was more than surprised, therefore, that when her confirmatory letter arrived it stated we had expressed a wish that the meeting be recorded without any reference to the fact that the proposal had emanated from Mr Coonan. The idea had not even entered our heads—I had simply said that if that was what Mr. Coonan wanted we would go along with it. I was very disappointed that after all the points we had made about the way we had been treated by the inquiry even a simple discussion of an administrative detail had not been correctly recorded. I rang Mrs Kent in protest emphasising how important it was to get things right. This elicited a letter in which Mrs Kent stated, 'I do apologise for any distress which you suggest has been incurred due to my letter to you. My note from our telephone conversation indicates that I advised you that Mr Coonan indicated that it would be helpful to have the meeting recorded, and that you indicated that that in fact was your wish also. It is that statement to which I referred in my letter and I was pleased to note that you were therefore in accordance with Mr Coonan's suggestion.'

We had submitted through our solicitors 65 questions we considered should be answered by the inquiry but by this stage we were again communicating direct with the inquiry rather than through lawyers. The North Essex Health Authority representing the commissioning agencies, had now taken on the responsibility for keeping us updated as to progress, reflecting (we guessed) a determination on their part to ensure they too were regularly updated.

We turned up for the meeting with the inquiry panel on November 21 in quite a different mood to our first meeting on June 7. We were on our own; we were not constrained by having a lawyer between us and the inquiry panel; we were not willing to allow the structure of the meeting to be imposed on us and our previous respect for the objectivity and authority of the panel had been destroyed. While we had changed we found no change in the inquiry for, despite the previous advice, when we entered the room we found the same layout we had experienced previously—not the informal gathering round a coffee table we had been led to expect!

The chairman took some time to explain the current state of the inquiry and invited Professor Bluglass to bring us up to date on the official thinking about inquiries. Through this we learned Professor Bluglass' university had organized a symposium about inquiries attended by members of previous inquiry panels; professionals who had been witnesses at inquiries and relatives of victims. They had not thought fit to invite us although we were directly involved in the most complex and expensive current inquiry and had made clear our concern about the way inquiries were conducted!

The chairman then held up the pages of 65 questions we had submitted and said that they went to the core of their investigation and all would be answered in the final report. He suggested we deal with our recommendations concerning the future of inquiries but we resisted, as a good deal of time had already been spent by the chairman and other members of the panel on generalities. We could foresee the possibility that the whole of the time allowed to us would be taken up by general issues and the main purpose of our meeting would be lost by our allotted time running out. We therefore pressed that we should start setting out the concerns we had with our dealings with this particular inquiry because our recommendations emerged from that experience.

We then went through our dissatisfaction about the sudden change in secretariat; being misled over whether hearings would be in public or private; no response to our questions about the process to be followed at the directions hearing; being misled about meeting the chairman to discuss procedural matters before meeting the inquiry panel; generally insensitive treatment; and so on. The chairman seemed uncomfortable with our insistence on going over the details of our unsatisfactory experiences, much of which—it occurred to us—may well have been news to the other panel members sitting alongside him.

We were polite, probably excessively so, but persistent and when Paul said that people did not perceive the inquiry to be independent because the secretariat was questioning witnesses who may be clients of their real estate business or members of the same lodge, rotary club or golf club, the chairman was provoked to a ringing endorsement of the support they had received from the secretariat. Later the chairman sought to move on saying that he did not think it was appropriate to review all that, which stung me into responding, 'Excuse me, I don't think it is appropriate to hold a review but I do think everyone ought to know our position precisely and what happened.'

Much of our comment was regarding our concerns with the inquiry but we also pressed the inquiry that they should interview the superintendent who was in overall charge of the initial police investigation and the inspector to investigate our allegation that we had been told that the two young men met in reception when police statements showed they had not. An inquiry which did not address conflict between what was known and what was told to us would in our view have failed. The chairman indicated they had not intended to interview these two but would consider our views. The chairman also repeated a statement he had made to our barrister at the first hearing and in subsequent correspondence that we would be invited to make submissions on a range of nominated matters; no such invitation was ever issued. We pressed too for access to the draft report when it became available.

By the end of the meeting we felt we had at least put our concerns about the inquiry process on the record though we were not so convinced the chairman and the inquiry panel were prepared to accept and deal with them. After the meeting we had a separate discussion with Mr Randall, the senior solicitor from Leonard Gray, who assured us of his total independence from any kind of local pressure. After this discussion had been going on for some time the chairman entered the room nominally to press Mr Randall to return to the meeting although it seemed to us the latter was rather dismissive of this request. The chairman also—rather haltingly for so fluent an individual—expressed his apologies. Our impression was that he had been pressed by his colleagues that we were entitled to an apology and rather reluctantly was carrying out their wishes.

As it was clear to us by now that both the commissioning agencies and the inquiry itself recognised and were embarrassed by their treatment of us which had forced us to incur legal expenses of approximately £2,400, we raised again the issue of reimbursement. On this occasion we gratefully acknowledge that the decision was taken to reimburse us by way of an *ex gratia* payment.

In order to press home the importance we attached to the inquiry panel interviewing the police who had investigated Christopher's death, we followed up our attendance by a final submission. In it we set out in detail the reasons why we regarded it essential they investigate and report on the way the agencies, primarily the Prison Service and the police, had reacted to the tragedy and treated ourselves. We considered it essential for the inquiry to investigate how the original statements by prison officers to the police that the two did not meet until placed in the same cell could be reconciled with our allegation that ten days later officers of both agencies were telling us the two had met in reception, formed a friendly relationship and that that was the reason they were in the same cell.

In due course the inquiry secretariat told us they had contacted the Essex police about an appearance by the superintendent and inspector. The police lawyers had challenged this as being beyond the terms of reference of the inquiry so the chairman had asked the agencies for their views on an extension of the terms of reference to cover this point.

We were disappointed but not surprised by the Essex police action. We immediately wrote to the chairman of the Essex Police Authority, the body which is supposed to monitor the police in the interests of the community, seeking its support for the proposal that the issue of whether the Prison Service and the police had been truthful in their dealings with us, which was important for the confidence of the community as well as ourselves, was investigated. This was of course the very same issue we had raised in our original draft of the terms of reference and later at the directions hearing and so we wrote again to the commissioning agencies asking them to agree that the points we had raised should be considered by the inquiry. We also sought the assistance of our MP and made similar representations to the Home Secretary because of his national responsibility for the police and because the Prison Service, responsible to him, was part sponsor of the inquiry.

Needless to say all the official responses to our representations were negative. Our impression was then and remains that the significance of the issue we were raising was recognised at the outset but that it was not considered acceptable for us to make public our belief and allegations of a cover up. To do so would expose a canker at the heart of the criminal justice system, leading to public criticism and possible court action. Similarly, none of the agencies, in our view, was willing to accept responsibility for blocking this line of investigation and invoking the terms of reference was simply to confuse the issue. The Essex police challenged whether the investigation we thought was necessary was within the terms of reference and the inquiry said it could not proceed unless the terms of reference were changed. The commissioning agents, however, said that while they would not change the terms of reference, it was for 'the inquiry panel to decide the extent to which they wished to inquire into the management action (by the various agencies) which subsequently took place.'

As a conventional, middle-class, middle-aged couple we felt dismayed by the performance of the public services which we had for most of our lives considered to be pillars of society. The impact on us was that when it came to a crisis the truth; sensitivity to individuals bereaved by such a tragedy and the community's need to learn the real lessons in order to help future generations would all be sacrificed to the self-protective interests of bureaucratic public institutions.

CHAPTER 14

Finding Friends ... and Others

The despair generated by our experience with the public agencies was countered by an unexpected joy which came from our participation in a service at St. Martin's-in-the-Fields shortly before Christmas 1996. This was arranged by Sandra Sullivan, whose daughter had been murdered by a paranoid schizophrenic at a Mind hostel where she had been a voluntary worker before going up to Oxford. Sandra, like Jayne Zito, Wendy Robinson and ourselves, was committed to identification of the truth and changing what needed to be changed. Somehow she had been able to arrange a service of recognition of the needs of the secondary victims of these tragedies: the families of those who had been killed. The most moving moment came when all those who had lost someone were invited to come forward and light a candle in their memory. There were many more people present than we had expected and the unexpected joy came from seeing over 100 candles lighting up the gloom of a dark winter morning. There was light in the darkness.

Though Paul and I belong to different Christian denominations we find great support in our religious life and often are able to worship together. When the first anniversary of Christopher's death occurred in 1995, it was a great help for us to go and spend a few days in retreat at Mount St Bernard's Abbey in Leicestershire. The accommodation and food were simple but the overall environment and our frequent daily attendances at the various offices of the day with traditional plainchant were most uplifting. The following year we went to Clare Priory nearby, which was much smaller and more intimate. Some of the services were of a more charismatic nature than we were used to. At the morning mass on November 29, the anniversary date, we were each invited to read passages from the Scriptures—a very sensitive gesture we thought.

We were thinking about where to go in 1997 when we received an invitation to appear on *Sunday Live*, a Sunday morning TV programme hosted by Gloria Hunniford. This was an invitation we did not consider we should reject for it seemed appropriate to remember Christopher by contributing to a programme in which by telling the story of his tragedy we could hope to bring help to others.

A heartwarming development resulted from our appearance on *Sunday Live:* I received a phone call a few days later from a young man who identified himself as Peter, a friend of Christopher's from the chess club. We were very surprised, as Christopher had never talked much about his evenings playing chess nor about any friends he had made there. Peter later came to see us and told us how he and other members had spent several weekends with Christopher at chess tournaments and said how well liked Christopher was at the club. Christopher was not the loner that some people may have believed: he was just very shy. It was so comforting to hear from a complete stranger that Christopher was so well regarded and perhaps more significantly that in all the time he attended the chess club and tournament weekends it was never apparent that he suffered a mental illness.

•　　•　　•

The personal impact of Christopher's tragedy, which went very deep, was something we found difficult to talk about—but we had no reservations about discussing changes in policy and practice which Christopher's tragedy had revealed the need for. Along with other families and carers we wanted to change mental health law and practice so that the mentally ill were looked after in the spirit of the Good Samaritan and not abandoned to survive on their own. We wanted also to raise the standard of treatment of prisoners. We were fearful of appearing as 'know-alls' on a publicity seeking exercise, but equally we recognised that we had experience of a tragedy and the early indifference and self-regard of the public institutions involved, from which lessons of benefit to the community could be obtained if there was a will to do so.

We were particularly incensed to read press reports of a policy document released by the Royal College of Psychiatrists. In it the college called for the abolition of inquiries such as we were involved in, on the grounds that they were expensive and damaged public confidence and staff morale. It should be sufficient, the college said, to rely on legal proceedings, disciplinary proceedings, inquests and the National Confidential Inquiry into Homicide and Suicides by Mentally Ill People.

We were appalled by the attitude of the psychiatric profession's official body, which we thought was characteristic of all the public agencies involved. They seemed only to see the issues from the point of view of the providers of the services and ignored the position of their clients whom they were supposed to serve, and their families. While we were critical of the way in which our inquiry was being carried out, the alternatives suggested by the Royal College would have been worse.

As we had found out, in the case of a homicide where the person pleads guilty to manslaughter there is no inquest and virtually no information about what happened is made public at the trial. Apart from anything else, this means there is little evidence on which to base legal proceedings. The National Inquiry is by definition confidential, as are disciplinary proceedings, and there is very little evidence of disciplinary proceedings being instigated sufficiently frequently to be an effective sanction. Psychiatrists, we concluded, were unwilling to have their peace of mind disturbed by public scrutiny of their failures and would prefer the community to be left in blissful ignorance by being denied information, rather than aroused by knowledge to demand improvements in this public service.

We had a similar disagreement with the Prison Governors' Association whose chairman made a public statement calling for offenders to be brought into face-to-face contact with their victims. We wrote applauding the principle of Restorative Justice he had proclaimed, adding that his argument would have carried greater conviction with us if prison officers acted in the same spirit towards prisoners and their families. We pointed out that the request we had made to meet with prison officers who had been responsible for Christopher had not been granted and we knew from contact with other families bereaved by a death in prison that they too had not received a decent response in face-to-face contact.

In mid-May 1997 we were informed by the agencies that the inquiry chairman had advised the report would be handed over in the first half of July and they promised to liaise with us about publication. Shortly afterwards the new Director General of the Prison Service, Richard Tilt, invited us to see him before publication. Mr Tilt was cordial, assured us he would not wish us to pull our punches on the release of the report, and suggested that it would be helpful if we were to address the Prison Governors' Conference about our experiences. We also raised with him other cases where families had told us they had not been treated properly by the Prison Service after they had been bereaved by a death in custody.

We then prepared for the promised release of the report by briefing local MPs; the media; voluntary organizations such as the Prison Reform Trust, the Prisoners' Advice Service and the Howard League; and also the offices of the Archbishop of Canterbury and Cardinal Hume because we felt it was essential the churches take the lead in calling for change. Some good outcomes flowed from these contacts but they were not related to the publication of the report. The promised handover by the chairman did not take place in July and was repeatedly deferred beyond the end of 1997.

Earlier in 1997 we had discovered that the Institute for the Study and Treatment of Delinquency (ISTD),[1] based at King's College London, was holding a conference on 'Deaths of Offenders' at Brunel University in July. Having pressed on them the need to recognise the position of families we found ourselves invited to hold a workshop. Julia Braggins and Stephanie Hayman of ISTD were highly supportive and sympathetic and their encouragement helped make our presentation go well. Later, at the suggestion of Chris Mullins MP, chairman of the House of Commons Select Committee on Home Affairs, we sent copies of the paper we gave at the workshop to each member of that committee. Another contact made at that conference was John Wadham, director of the civil rights organization

---

[1] Now the Centre for Crime and Justice Studies.

Liberty, to whom Paul had already spoken on the phone. This contact proved to be of great significance later.

During the conference we had the opportunity of meeting with some good and dedicated prison officers, who acknowledged to us that they fully accepted all that we had said about the way the Prison Service had treated first Christopher and then ourselves and were ashamed. The bureaucratic face of the Prison Service was also present as we were introduced to the then Deputy Director General, Tony Pearson. We noted that he was scheduled to attend our session and as we waited in the conference room to begin we observed him pass the glass door a number of times. In the end he did not attend, telling us later he regretted he had been delayed by business calls.

We met Mr Pearson again in August, together with some of his colleagues, at a meeting arranged to take further the Director General's suggestion that we talk to the Prison Governors' conference. The official view at this meeting was that while a contribution about our experience could be useful, their annual conference was not the most appropriate event for this. There was an evident lack of enthusiasm to pursue the idea and nothing further was heard about making use of our experience until much later, after a major change in senior personnel at the top of the Prison Service.

We did, on the other hand, have a much more constructive meeting with the representatives of the two churches. Hosted by Charles Wookey in Cardinal Hume's office, it was also attended by the Reverend Dr Peter Sedgwick, Assistant Secretary of the Church of England Board of Social Responsibility. We got to know Peter Sedgwick better as a key figure promoting a positive commitment by the churches to change attitudes towards the criminal justice system. He also helped to give us an introduction to the *Church Times* which later published a substantial and sympathetic coverage of issues involved. Anita Dockley, the very helpful representative of the Howard League whom we had briefed in anticipation of publication of the report, had arranged for us to make a presentation at the Howard League Conference in September. The presentation on our experience was well received by those who attended.

This series of interactions was carried out against a background of continued deferrals of the date of release of the inquiry report, which was constantly being revised but was always two or three months away! One consequence, which we thought unacceptable, was that publication was delayed beyond the three-year limit on taking legal action for negligence. The repeated delays appeared now to be an irritant to the commissioning agents who doubtless shared our frustration and were urging expeditious completion. Our periodic visits to the library revealed that the minutes of the Essex County Council Social Services Committee showed that whereas it had originally been estimated that the total cost of the inquiry would be £300,000, sittings had continued longer than expected incurring additional costs. The total cost was now estimated at £770,000. Further delays and cost increases were yet to become evident.

We were told the draft report would first be released to the agencies for them to check but we could not see the text until the final report was published. We argued strongly that it was contrary to natural justice to allow the agencies, who were at fault, to see and comment on the draft but to deny it to both ourselves and Richard Linford's family. We made strong representations about this and understood the elected members from all parties on the Essex County Council, one of the three sponsors of the inquiry, supported our appeal, as did our MP. We gained the impression that another sponsor, the North Essex Health Authority, was also sympathetic. We concluded that the third sponsor, the Home Office, was opposed and, as a result, we would be denied access to the draft—which made us angry and disappointed.

•   •   •

As so often happened during our dealings with the inquiry, an apparent defeat turned into a victory: a major error we would have picked up in the draft was carried forward to the published report and we were able to use it later as evidence to demonstrate the failure of the inquiry on an important issue.

We did learn, from a letter to our solicitors from the chairman of the inquiry, that its title and presumably the substance had changed significantly. It was no longer an investigation into Christopher's death, as had been made clear in the original ministerial statements, the press release, the terms of reference, and in all previous contacts with the chairman and inquiry secretariat. It was now called 'An Inquiry into the Care and Treatment of Christopher Edwards and Richard Linford', thus giving primacy to the responsibilities—and failings—of the health and social services rather than of the police, courts and Prison Service. We objected, but to no avail.

The protracted delay in publication was not just a cause of concern to ourselves and the agencies. It was by now quite frequently referred to by the local media who contacted us for our views on the delay as well as on other local issues, for example, when the Chief Inspector of Prisons published a critical report on Chelmsford Prison.

•   •   •

Earlier in the process, when we had been at our most despairing, we had contacted the Max Clifford organization for possible assistance. While this was not a case they wished to follow up they did helpfully give us a name to contact at the *Guardian*, to whom the *Church Times* journalist had also referred our case. The *Guardian* sent a reporter, Sarah Boseley, to obtain the story and we agreed to pick her up at the nearby railway station and bring her home to tell her the full story and show her the documents. The result was a very powerful article in the *Guardian*.[2]

There was one very unexpected outcome from the *Guardian* article. Sarah Boseley forwarded to us a letter she had received from a prisoner who had been in Chelmsford Prison at the time of Christopher's death and who was willing to talk about it. Knowing that his letter would be read by prison officers, the prisoner had written in carefully guarded terms as if he was writing a personal letter to an old friend about an incident in a hotel in which he had been staying. Not wishing to put him at any risk of retribution, we responded in equally guarded terms and arranged to visit him. We dressed as inconspicuously as possible and experienced the queueing and stringent security checks at the prison.

When our prisoner arrived at the nominated table in the meeting hall he made it clear he had no direct knowledge about what happened to Christopher but said he had been involved in a serious attack on another prisoner the night following Christopher's death. He had been charged for this attack but contrary to his and other prisoners' expectations the case against him was dismissed. The most plausible explanation was that the prison did not wish to acknowledge there had been another serious cell incident the night after Christopher's death.

We have maintained contact with him since then, visiting him again in other prisons and sending the occasional letter. He is an artistically talented young man who appears to have worked through his youthful folly and we would expect him to be a good citizen on release, provided he is not driven back to crime by prejudice against employing him because of his criminal past.

• • •

A letter in our daily paper from a prison visitor about the national failure to deal properly with the mentally ill who are sent to prison prompted us to respond to him directly. He put us in touch with Dr Deborah Cheney, then editor of a quarterly magazine for members of Boards of Visitors, who invited us to write an article which was published under the heading 'A Prison Service which Lied to Us'. This in turn led to contact with Mark Leech, an ex-prisoner dedicated to reform of the Prison Service and providing assistance to prisoners and ex-prisoners. He is joint editor of the annual *The Prisons Handbook* (TPH) and a co-founder of Unlock—the National Association of Ex-Offenders. We were very touched when later he asked whether we would agree to the 1999 edition of *The Prisons Handbook* being dedicated to Christopher. We readily agreed.

---

[2]   6 January 1998.

About this time we attended a conference on mental health in prisons. The conference was aimed at professionals in the mental health and criminal justice fields, who were all charged a substantial fee. We pointed out to the organizers that we had a significant interest in the issue but could not afford the fee out of our pocket. The organizers helpfully enabled us to attend anyway.

Two things stand out in my memory from that conference: the first was a statement by a senior consultant forensic psychiatrist, speaking from a platform on which were sitting Dr John Reed (Medical Inspector, HM Inspectorate of Prisons and the author of a major report on mental health in prisons) and the then Director of Healthcare for the Prison Service. The psychiatrist said that although his professional colleagues would kill him for spilling the beans, it was well established practice for psychiatrists to seek to send their most difficult clients to prison rather than to hospital. None of the experts on the platform or in the hall in any way challenged or questioned this statement; they had, perhaps, long known it to be true whereas we had only recently discovered it.

My second recollection is the warm and hearty applause Paul received when he stood up and challenged the professionals there, saying they were all too complacent in accepting that mentally ill people had been sent to prison for years and that the standard of prison healthcare was inadequate. They should, he said, be doing something to change this, not just talking about it, and they should recognise the impact it had on the individuals concerned and their families. Such a response showed we were right in our assessment of what had happened and encouraged us to believe there would be support from many of the professionals involved, if only the government were prepared to face up to the difficulties and make a policy decision that change was required

•   •   •

At last, after much despair, we seemed to be seeing some light at the end of a long tunnel. With the help of others we felt we might be able to achieve something positive from Christopher's tragedy; to give his life meaning so that it should not seen as a terrible waste. We felt that the path could only now proceed upwards, albeit not without its struggles.

CHAPTER 15

The Whole Truth and Nothing But?

As the date for the release of the inquiry report[1] drew nearer we no longer had the high hopes we had entertained at the outset that it would reveal the truth in full. We realised that it would be necessary to encourage extensive coverage by the media if the truth—as we understood it—was to be revealed. We also realised that we needed some professional advice on public relations if we were to ensure that the community would understand the true story rather than accept the institutional damage control exercise which by this time we feared the report would amount to.

We went to the public library, noted down the details of half-a-dozen PR agencies and wrote asking if they were prepared to advise us on a *pro bono* basis. Not all replied but those that did offered constructive advice. One in particular—Peter Chandler—saw us on more than one occasion and advised on the content of our documentation and proposed means of conveying it to the community. This generous and positive support was in sharp contrast to the popular image of the cynical PR consultant.

David Johnson, chief executive of the North Essex Health Authority, together with two of his staff, Peter Greenwood and Amanda Westbrook, showed us genuine sympathy and support. Amanda was very helpful, particularly when it became apparent that the effect of the stress was damaging my health. She arranged for me see a well-respected local counselling service. Though very well intentioned the counselling sessions did not help. I am not by nature talkative, least of all about my internal concerns, but the whole focus appeared to be based on a capacity to 'let it all hang out'. During the third session there were several rather long and embarrassed silences after which both the counsellor and I agreed that no useful purpose would be served by continuing. However, at one point I had related to the counsellor the nightmares I had been having and the strange dreams of Christopher, which were very vivid. I was greatly relieved to be reassured that I was not going mad! One of my most poignant dreams of Christopher was that he walked through the door and said, 'I know you're worried about me, Mum, but I'm all right really.' This brought a sort of peace but I knew that peace of mind would never really come until the truth was known and acknowledged by all concerned.

At the end of November 1997 our regular visits to the reference section in the library revealed that the North Essex Health Authority had recorded in their minutes their concerns at the delay in producing the report and

---

[1] *Report of the Inquiry into the Care and Treatment of Christopher Edwards and Richard Linford: A Report Commissioned by North Essex Health Authority, Essex County Council and HM Prison Service in association with Essex Police* (2001). Available from the health authority.

their decision to send a stern letter to the inquiry chairman demanding the precise reasons for the delay. This move, it was recorded, was supported by the Department of Health. To all appearances, it seemed that the agencies had suffered from a similar experience with the chairman as we had and we hoped that—if necessary—they were as prepared to be critical of the text of the report as they were of the process of producing it.

Recognising that the medical details of Christopher's death were likely to be particularly traumatic the health authority suggested to us that it might be beneficial for the Director of Public Health to take us through them well in advance.

On a bright sunny day in April we turned up with Clare to hear the distressing story in detail. Dr Carroll and Amanda Westbrook were very sensitive in the way they explained what had happened during the frenzied attack on Christopher. Dr Carroll quoted references in the draft report and also his own investigations into Christopher's death. The key piece of information we gathered was Dr Carroll's advice, following consultation with a specialist consultant, that the most significant factor causing Christopher's death was an injury to the throat affecting the flow of blood and oxygen to the brain. Neither the timing of this injury nor of Christopher's death could be determined precisely. The Home Office pathologist apparently was quoted in the report as saying that it was unlikely Christopher could have been resuscitated even if prison officers had entered the cell, but clearly if the blow causing the critical injury had happened at the conclusion of the attack it is possible Christopher's life might have been saved if prison officers had entered the cell as soon as the assault was discovered. While it was impossible to achieve absolute certainty on the issue, we thought both opinions were equally valid and that in the interests of balance and integrity both should be included in the report. Reliance on the Home Office pathologist alone did, of course, have the effect of protecting the Home Office and Prison Service from criticism

We were also distressed by the blurring of why Christopher's ear could not be traced. While it was revolting to have to acknowledge that his ear might have been cannibalised, what actually happened was very important to us. We felt it would have been better to deal with the issue in the text of the report rather than relegate it to the insignificance of a footnote.

We asked the health authority to convey to the chairman our strong view that the draft should be modified to take these comments into account, but in the event it failed to mention the alternative medical explanation and the issue of the missing ear remained as a footnote.

•   •   •

About this time we had a meeting with the agencies at which the proposed arrangements for the release of the report were explained: we were to have three days to read the report in the health authority's offices. We took the opportunity at this meeting to raise the possibility of a multi-agency supported project in memory of Christopher, such as a bail hostel for mentally disturbed offenders. We also suggested there could be benefit in a jointly sponsored training video for staff in which we were willing to participate and the agencies undertook to consider this.

It was finally agreed that the inquiry report would be released on 15 June 1998 and we would be able to read it in the health authority's offices from June 10. We took up the invitation and with Clare attended to read the 324 pages with their eleven appendices and 85 recommendations. After waiting so long for this, it was a curious experience to arrive at an office block and within its impersonal surroundings to read the thousands of words of cold print about the most personally disturbing experience of our lives.

I was greatly taken aback to find the colour of the cover of the report was burgundy. I had thought about the colour I would prefer, though we had never been consulted, and burgundy would have been the colour of my choice; the burgundy would be symbolic of Christopher's blood, and the white lettering of his gentle soul. Again, a very emotional moment.

Paul recollects that the contrast between the poignant tragedy of Christopher's death and the mundane report was highlighted for him when, while reading the report, he became aware of a conversation coming through the office wall about the apparently serious issue that one member of the inquiry wanted his wife to be present at the final press conference to launch the report and this caused difficulties because there was not enough space, and another member had had to be told his son could not attend. What was for us a deeply personal and tragic experience was, it would seem, for some an opportunity to participate in a media spectacle!

We did not find the document itself very impressive; the length and copious recommendations reflected, we thought, a wish to justify its by now £1 million cost and three-year time frame rather than the profundity of its analysis. As we had expected from the time we noted the change in the heading on letters from the inquiry, the report focused on the care and treatment of the two young men and only investigated the details of the homicide superficially, giving little attention to the subsequent behaviour of the Prison Service and police in their dealings with us. The whole tone, it seemed to us, was one of bland acceptance of the inevitability of such tragedies; insofar as anyone was held responsible it was Christopher and Richard because they had failed to take their medication!

Much of the content of the report was already known to us because we had read all of the statements taken by the police. We did learn for the first time that when previously held in Norwich Prison Richard Linford had said voices were telling him to kill his cellmate and that when he was in Chelmsford Prison on a previous occasion his mental condition was so disturbing that the visiting prison psychiatrist pressed for his immediate transfer to secure psychiatric accommodation at Runwell Hospital. One of the most horrific findings was that on the night of the tragedy the cell alarm had been activated but did not work—with a strong inference that this may have been because it had been rendered inoperative by the insertion of a matchstick on the outside of the cell.[2]

We also learned that prison staff had made a written list of the names of the inmates of the other cells on the same landing of the prison where the tragedy took place. It could not, however, be produced to the inquiry because it had been lost. The investigating police officers had also made a list of cell inmates but this could not be produced because, by an amazing coincidence, it too had been lost.

A key question we had put to the inquiry was why the two young men had been placed in the same cell when the prison officers were aware that both were mentally ill and Richard was known to be violent. This was answered very simply: the officer concerned did not think Richard would hurt Christopher! This is despite the fact that the same officer had said '[Richard] was not fit to go in with other inmates' and the recollection by reception staff of Richard's behaviour on his previous stay in the prison.

We took it in turns to go and read the report because there were three of us and only two copies. Paul was a systematic reader, beginning at the front and working his way through, whilst I looked at the sections in which I was particularly interested. One afternoon when I was there with Clare I was shocked to discover that while it was acknowledged that Essex police and the Prison Service had given us the same incorrect explanation about what had happened, the inquiry, which claimed to have investigated the matter carefully, explained it away as a misunderstanding of a Prison Service internal investigation report.

I was deeply disappointed and depressed by this. Fortunately, on his next visit Paul's systematic reading identified an internal contradiction in the text which completely undermined this conclusion. We checked our files to confirm the report's explanation could not be right and decided one priority would be to highlight this contradictory evidence at the press conference. We recalled wryly the sustained refusal of our repeated requests to see the draft report. If we had been allowed to see the draft we would certainly have pointed out this error and saved Mr Coonan the embarrassment we caused by pointing it out at the press conference!

On another occasion while attending the health authority's offices to read the report, I met Richard's mother, and we had a long talk about our children—as mothers often do. She told me many sad accounts of Richard's illness and how when he was well he was a very different person. Why did those responsible for Richard have to wait until he killed someone for him

---

[2] We wrote about this in *Deaths of Offenders: The Hidden Side of Justice* (1998), Liebling, A (ed), Winchester: Waterside Press. It is dealt with in the report at 1479-1494, see esp. 1488: 'We cannot rule out the possibility that [the audible warning system] had been deliberately tampered with before 28 November 1994'; and 1490: 'This investigation has revealed a very serious defect . . . which may also apply in other prisons . . . it is essential that the emergency cell call system operates properly at all times'.

to receive the treatment and care he so desperately needed? Compulsory medication to prevent a homicide is surely to be preferred to waiting for a homicide before insisting on medication.

•　　•　　•

Meanwhile, we also had a very busy time being interviewed by the press, radio and several TV news channels prior to the official release of the report. On publication day the health authority provided us with maximum support, including a room for our private use and a member of staff to sort out any administrative issues. The press conference launch was held in the same Essex County Council committee room as the initial directions hearing. As we had discovered from the overheard conversation at the health authority's offices space was limited and attendance was by invitation. When we arrived we found Michael Howlett, director of the Zito Trust, waiting outside but without an invitation, so we suggested he join our party in our private room. When we went into the committee room Michael slipped away into the general throng of the media. They were arranged in tiered ranks, with the first rank being the sound media, behind which was a battery of TV cameras and then the press. All the available seats were occupied and many people were standing at the back of the room: quite a crowd.

In his introductory remarks the chairman of the North Essex Health Authority, Alec Sexton, issued a general apology on behalf of all the agencies concerned for failing both families. The inquiry panel chairman then spoke, and he and other panel members answered questions. Then representatives of the various agencies went through the same process. One journalist asked the Deputy Director General of the Prison Service why the night duty officer who had been the last to pass the cell had not been required by the Prison Service to give evidence to the inquiry. He responded, 'That was his choice.' This seemed a lamentable failure by the Prison Service to encourage their staff to assist the inquiry on a fundamental issue and was a statement I found quite difficult to accept.

It was our turn next and we were to be followed by Richard Linford's mother and sister. We had agreed that each of us would speak so I began, followed by Paul and then Clare. For the sake of politeness we acknowledged the detailed exposition of the long history of unremitting failure by all the agencies involved in treating both young men. Then we criticised the report for the acceptance of the tragic inevitability of failure and for the omissions and interpretation of evidence which, we felt, gave a misleading picture.

Our major criticism was directed at the inquiry's failure to investigate properly why the Essex police and the Prison Service had given us an incorrect explanation of events after the tragedy. We pointed out the impossibility of the inquiry's explanation, i.e. that the Prison Service had misinterpreted the report of the investigation by the Governor of Norwich Prison and this misinterpretation had been passed on to the police. We pointed out that this explanation could not be true because the incorrect explanation had been conveyed to us in person by the Essex police on December 9 and by the Prison Service in writing on the same date, yet the inquiry report stated explicitly that the Norwich Prison Governor's report was not completed until December 16. Moreover, the police knew the truth from the statements they had taken on November 29 and it would be wholly against police practice for them to rely on evidence from a third party when they had their own records to rely on.

We then argued that the facts showed that mental health legislation needed to be strengthened so that the medical authorities should intervene positively to assist mentally ill people in need of treatment who did not recognise their own condition, and that the practice of dumping the most disturbed mentally ill people in prison should be abandoned.

Finally, Clare emphasised the need for all public agencies to give much greater recognition to the needs of families than we had experienced. She suggested that as all the agencies had failed, they had a debt of obligation to Christopher which they could repay by establishing a much needed new psychiatric facility named after him. Finally she argued that the substantial cost and time involved in this inquiry would be wasted unless positive action was taken following it.

When Richard Linford's mother spoke, she was overtaken by emotion as she conveyed her own and Richard's sorrow at what had happened. I was sitting next to her and felt deeply touched, so I instinctively stretched out my hand to comfort her: a moment of unity in grief for our lost sons.

The formal session was followed by a hectic series of interviews with each of the TV, radio and newspaper journalists. Paul had to repeat the performance later in the day when he returned to Chelmsford to be interviewed live on *Channel 4 News*, sitting isolated in a studio being spoken to from afar.

• • •

On returning home I remember feeling absolutely exhausted and indeed quite ill. The strain had certainly taken its toll. I felt as though I was just recovering from a severe illness and it took two or three days to get back to normal. Clare too was under strain but Paul as ever remained a tower of strength.

CHAPTER 16

Putting the Record Straight

At the outset we had assumed the publication of the inquiry report would mark the end of the story. Now we realised this could not be. Too many of the 65 questions we had submitted to the inquiry remained unanswered and we feared the impetus for change might slacken if the agencies were not required to address the failings which had been revealed and public interest in the treatment of the mentally ill and prisoners was not maintained.

We decided that we must do our best to put the record straight. The issues were important to us; we knew most of the facts; and we had had contact with the inquiry and the three commissioning agencies as well as with other families affected by similar tragedies. By now the police had released to us the official statements, including those given to the internal police inquiry but they did not add much to what we knew already. To say we 'decided' is not quite accurate: we did not feel we had a choice to make but were driven to do what we could. Both Paul and I sat down to read the inquiry report again, comparing it with our records and our experience, making careful notes which we discussed before preparing our own written assessment of it.

First we considered the defects in the inquiry process. Public records showed that the commissioning agencies and the Department of Health shared our concerns over the delays, which Essex County Council said had 'increased the level of injustice for the Edwards and Linford families', and the cost which had tripled from an initial estimate of some £300,000 to around £1 million. The council was so disturbed that it resolved that its concerns should be made known to the Secretary of State for Health and the Local Government Association.

After setting out the insensitive way in which we felt we had been treated by the inquiry we noted that the report acknowledged that the Prison Service and investigating police had erroneously advised us the two young men had met in the prison reception area. The inquiry, which said it examined this issue closely, stated that it was likely that this error arose out of a misunderstanding of the internal investigation report by Governor Fowler. We pointed out this could not be so because another paragraph stated that Governor Fowler's report was handed in on 16 December 1994, whereas the erroneous statements by both agencies were made to us before then.[1]

---

[1] See and compare 1416 and 1438 in the inquiry report.

We then listed variances between the inquiry report and the evidence submitted. Though not all of those variances were of equal significance, they suggested to us a somewhat cavalier and superficial attitude to accuracy given the very serious nature of the events under consideration. We had been surprised, for example, when reading the report to see ourselves quoted as having said that the responses to us by the NHS Trust and the health authority had been 'open, detailed and prompt'. On checking our original submission we found that we had actually said the responses from these agencies were 'considerably more detailed, open and prompt than the responses by the Prison Service and the police.' By selecting only part of a quotation the inquiry had changed the meaning of our original statement. Another example which we found quite offensive was the report's attribution of rather coarse language to Christopher in the magistrates' court. Paul had been present throughout and did not hear any of the alleged language, nor was it recorded by any of the police in statements taken at the time.

We then sought to identify examples of questionable judgements within the inquiry report. The most significant of these, which was completely at variance with reality and commonsense, was its interpretation of the statement by the prison officer who, when placing Richard in a cell on his own, had said he was 'unfit to go in with other inmates'. This officer apparently told the inquiry (see inquiry report 1439) that by those words he meant that Richard might be injured by other prisoners if he remained with them in the reception area and he did not think he posed any risk to Christopher. His attempt to absolve himself from blame for transferring Richard into the cell occupied by Christopher, whom he had said earlier should be in a cell on his own 'for his own protection', was understandable if not plausible—but incredibly the inquiry chose to accept his retrospective self-justification at face value. This was despite the fact that the inquiry panel knew that in his statement the same prison officer had said he had been warned Richard was 'potentially a problem as he had been fighting and causing trouble at the court earlier in the day.'

We gave another example in the many references to the psychiatrist principally responsible for Richard Linford. The report did identify shortcomings, e.g. that he had not carried out a systematic risk assessment (643); had consistently played down the amount of risk (643); failed to communicate decisions (788); and continued to hold a mistaken view of the risk presented by Richard (890). We contrasted these with the judgement 'that he was a conscientious and caring psychiatrist'! (892) We concluded with suggestions based on our experience of how such inquiries could be conducted in a way sensitive to the needs of families involved.

We had intended to send a copy of our views to all who had received the original report. By the time we completed our review, in October, we had received feedback from a number of sources that the inquiry report was not rated as highly as the three-years and £1 million cost should have guaranteed. We heard many comments about the report some of which were quite disparaging. We decided it was not necessary to circulate our own view of a report which had already been judged and found wanting. We did, however, send copies to a range of interested parties including the commissioning agencies. They asked if we would agree to copies being sent to the members of the panel, to which we readily gave consent on condition that any comments they made were passed back to us. We never received any such comments.

•   •   •

We felt compelled to continue to seek a proper investigation of the reason why we had been given an incorrect version of what happened by the Prison Service and the police. We pressed for a statutory judicial inquiry in public and wanted to raise the matter directly with the Home Secretary but our new MP, Alan Hurst (who had replaced Tony Newton at the 1997 election) suggested we meet the Minister for Prisons, Joyce Quinn. A meeting was arranged but on the day before there was a ministerial reshuffle and she was transferred elsewhere. The new minister was Lord Williams of Mostyn and in due course we went to visit him with Alan Hurst. We were shown into an ante-room to await being called. It was a tense period, but then Lord Williams quickly dispelled my anxieties with his sympathetic manner. It was, however, clear there was no wish by the minister or the Home Office to set up a judicial inquiry, although he did suggest we approach the Parliamentary Ombudsman. Alan Hurst agreed with Lord Williams that this would be the best way forward and we agreed to consider this suggestion.

Upon reflection Paul and I decided to proceed with a complaint to the Ombudsman because that was the only option. Five months later the Ombudsman reported that he 'found fully justified the complaint by Mr and Mrs Edwards that the Prison Service had misled them as to some of the circumstances which had led to the death in custody of their son'. He found that the Prison Service had allowed the wrong statement given to us to stand even though their internal inquiry clearly indicated a significantly different explanation was in order. The effect he said was 'to maintain a false impression concerning the possible extent of the Prison Service's culpability regarding the death well beyond the point at which the existence of that impression could legitimately be ascribed to an incomplete understanding of events'. The then Director General, Richard Tilt, was required to apologise to us and to release to us the internal inquiry report by Governor Fowler. To clarify the position fully we also asked for a copy of the initial internal report by Governor Sinclair which we also received.

We were relieved at last to have official confirmation that HM Prison Service had misled us and to receive an apology for that, but we did not think the Parliamentary Ombudsman had gone far enough. He suggested the wrong information was given to us initially because of a misinterpretation of the internal investigation reports and criticised the Prison Service for not correcting this situation later when the position was clearly understood. Now that we had access to those reports we could see they were clear and accurate and unlikely to be misunderstood, particularly in the context of a rare and serious incident such as a prison homicide. This, coupled with the refusal of an experienced prison Governor to make direct contact with us, despite the established policy on contact with bereaved relatives, was also, we thought, very suspicious.

As it happened we had by then met the chairman of the local Board of Visitors who had been called to the prison at the time of the tragedy. She told us she had impressed on the governor how important it was to visit us and explain the situation as sensitively as possible. She was incredulous when we told her that despite her urging otherwise neither he nor anyone else from the prison had visited us at the time. While we had received no visitors, the prison chaplain had gone to see Richard Linford's mother.

All of this together with the fact that both the Prison Service and the Essex police had, as the inquiry report acknowledged, given us the same inaccurate version of events even though it was contrary to the facts established in the statements taken by the police, made us go back to the Ombudsman. In his reply he at least acknowledged that the question whether there had been an intention to deceive, as we believed, or misinformation arising out of a muddle was something which could not be known for sure and must remain a matter of opinion. Perhaps we should be grateful that we achieved what we did.

One issue we raised which the Ombudsman did not take up was that we were not the only people to have been misled about what happened. So also had our MP, who had raised the issue on our behalf, and the then Conservative Home Secretary, Michael Howard, who had signed the letter to our MP. We had pointed out to the Ombudsman that it was not possible for ministers to have confidence in advice from civil servants or for MPs to have confidence in responses to representations on behalf of their constituents if cases such as ours, where wrong advice was given, are not identified and publicly condemned. We wrote to Michael Howard. He replied saying our allegations were serious and he thought it right to refer them to the Home Office through the then Labour Home Secretary, Jack Straw, for comment. We understood this and awaited his further contact after he received a reply from the Home Office. Mr Howard had sent his letter to the Home Secretary on 3 June 1999 and we assumed he would receive a reply fairly quickly. We were astonished to discover that he had to wait five months, until November 5, for that reply.

Mr Howard offered to discuss the matter with us personally and we accepted. We had been invited by the Revd. Dr Peter Sedgwick, the assistant secretary of the Church of England Board of Social Responsibility, to attend a book launch on November 9 of *Prisons: A Study in Vulnerability*, a collection of essays sponsored by the Board, which included an edited version of the article on Christopher's story from the *Church Times*. The book was to be launched by Lord Hurd of Westwell[2] in the House of Lords and I had been kindly invited to say a few words. The occasion was chaired by the Bishop of Lincoln and Lord Hurd gave a potent address on the shortcomings of the prison system. It seemed sensible to try and arrange a visit to Mr Howard at Westminster for the same day and fortunately he was able to spare us some time from his busy schedule.

• • •

We were greeted in the central hallway by Michael Howard's secretary and escorted through the labyrinth that is Westminster to his office: a small but comfortable room at the top of several flights of stairs. He immediately made it clear that as Home Secretary at the time he accepted ultimate responsibility for Christopher's death and apologised to us for it. He was sympathetic and attentive to our concerns and in no way resembled the public image of the hard-right extremist 'with a touch of the night about him'. If anything he conveyed the image of being something of a soft touch in that he found it hard to accept that a Civil Service in which he placed absolute trust would knowingly prepare a letter containing falsehoods for him to sign.

On reading Mr Straw's reply we were shocked to find the initial statement to us by the Prison Service that internal investigations revealed no serious defects, which the Ombudsman said was a serious misrepresentation meriting criticism, was described as a matter entirely within the proper remit of the Prison Service to reach its own conclusion! So, was it for the Prison Service to tell untruths if it so decided?

Mr Howard agreed that Mr Straw's letter did not answer the questions asked. In discussing what to do next, he said he was quite ready to raise the matter in an adjournment debate in the House of Commons but suggested that this was likely to be misrepresented as an attempt by him to attack Derek Lewis whom he had sacked as Director General. We agreed that it would be better if we wrote again to Mr Howard about the response received from the Home Office, so that he could forward this with his own queries to Jack Straw. We wrote as agreed, adding that we thought apologies to him from the Home Office and Prison Service for misleading him when Home Secretary would resolve the matter and establish that the precedent of misleading a minister who was responding to an MP raising a constituency issue was to be condemned and not followed.

---

[2] Lord Hurd is president of the Prison Reform Trust (PRT) and the Bishop of Lincoln was then the bishop for prisons.

A reply to Mr Howard's second letter was still awaited when in March 2000 we had a meeting with Martin Narey, the newly appointed Director General of the Prison Service. We brought up the issue of Mr Howard when Home Secretary being misled by the Prison Service and said that in our opinion Mr Howard was entitled to a letter of apology. Much to his credit, Mr Narey wrote a letter to Mr Howard in which he unreservedly apologised for the Prison Service's failure in submitting information which was incorrect and misleading. Jack Straw, the current Home Secretary, also conveyed his apologies to both Mr Howard and ourselves for the mishandling of the correspondence and for the fact that both parties had been provided with incorrect information in 1995. Mr Straw was quite genuine in expressing that he was 'very, very sorry about what happened in this case'. We appreciated the Home Secretary's candour in conveying this apology and readily accepted it.

We were not, however, wholly convinced by one part of Mr Straw's letter in which he said that when the then Director General wrote to us on 9 December 1994 with the inaccurate information officials would have been aware of the substance of the report by Governor Fowler. The reason for our doubt was that although the inquiry report stated the area manager had immediately appointed Governor Fowler to conduct the inquiry and that her report was submitted on December 16, the copy of the report sent to us by the Director General had attached to it the area manager's commissioning memo which was dated December 16 and required the findings by December 21.[3] As we were to discover also, the area manager later claimed not to have been involved in the correspondence sent to us.[4]

Somewhat to our surprise Michael Howard emerged from our contacts with him as a person of greater integrity and humanity than his public image might suggest.

---

[3] This appears to add further confusion to official versions of events: see footnote 1 on page 87 in relation to the inquiry report. Whichever version is looked at, something is clearly amiss.

[4] See page 101 of this book.

CHAPTER 17

Pinning Down Responsibility

We were convinced that in addition to identifying the failures which led to the tragedy, the individuals concerned should be made to accept responsibility. It was not a question of vengeance but of establishing on the record that such failures were not acceptable. If this was not done there would be no disincentive to repetition of the same or similar failures and some other son might suffer the same fate as Christopher. There was already evidence from Chelmsford Prison of a failure to learn the lessons of the tragedy. Members of HM Chief Inspector of Prisons' investigation team while on a prison inspection had pressed cell alarms repeatedly; while they had not been sabotaged or immobilised no officer responded to the calls.[1] The agencies had not indicated any intention to take disciplinary action after the publication of the inquiry report, so we concluded there was no option but to invoke the formal complaint processes for each agency.

Prior to the publication of the inquiry report we had attended the annual public meeting of the NHS Trust and asked whether it would take disciplinary action against any persons who had demonstrably failed. We were assured it was prepared to do so. After the report was published we asked the trust to take action against the two psychiatrists who, in our view, carried the major responsibility for the failures of the NHS in this case. In addition to the evidence in the report we asked them to take into account a memorandum by Inspector Robertson who had been at the case conference on Richard Linford in which he said

> The main impression I got from the meeting was that Linford was unlikely to be admitted to the Linden Centre at Chelmsford because he was too violent and could leave at any time. A number of psychiatric specialists had declined to section him so that he could be detained in secure accommodation because they did not feel it was merited on the evidence that they had. You will see from the minutes that a certain expectation was placed on me to find a way of having Linford placed in prison as an alternative. I was surprised that members of the medical profession felt that this was practicable or desirable.

The NHS Trust declined to take any disciplinary action or consider this memorandum because it said it should be guided solely by the inquiry report. At one stage the trust showed us a table demonstrating that many of those employed by it at the time of Christopher's tragedy were no longer so employed—as evidence of how it had changed. We discovered later that

---

[1] For a summary of this highly critical report in which healthcare for the mentally ill is also described as still being 'wholly inadequate' see *The Prisons Handbook* (2000 edition), Leech M and Cheney D (eds.), Winchester: Waterside Press.

one of the two psychiatrists against whom we had complained but who had then left the trust was subsequently re-employed! We also made it clear that we would welcome the opportunity of meeting the psychiatrists we had criticised, but no meeting was ever arranged.

Having failed to make any impact on the employers of the medical professionals we made a formal complaint to the General Medical Council. It took some time to reach a conclusion but eventually we were informed that the GMC was concerned at the standard of their practice though it did not consider it necessary to review either doctor's registration. The GMC had sent a statement of its concerns to the doctors who had also been advised as to their future conduct. The GMC had at least been willing to take action—albeit it seemed a fairly light rap on the knuckles—whereas the NHS Trust had not, so some progress had been made. We were astonished to discover that the NHS Trust had not been advised by the GMC of these professional decisions about the quality of performance of their employees. How could GMC decisions be an effective sanction to ensure better performance if they were not so disclosed? We sought to remedy this defect by sending the NHS Trust a copy of the letter we had received from the GMC. An interesting aspect of the GMC findings was that they criticised the senior psychiatrist for his inability to foster a proper working relationship with the social worker and the other professionals concerned.

Initially we had been told that a complaint about performance by a magistrates' court had to be made to the Lord Chancellor's office, which we did. Then we were advised it had to be made to the local magistrates' courts committee (MCC). Asking magistrates and court officers to pass judgement on colleagues with whom they have a day-to-day working relationship does not appear to be a very independent or objective appeal process. But it was the only one available, so we used it. Our complaint was based on statements in the inquiry report that court officers believed that Christopher required a psychiatric assessment and that there was a real possibility he was acutely mentally ill, one magistrate having described him as being in 'a highly mentally disordered state.' The report went on to say: 'The bench expressed its concern about Christopher Edwards' personal safety in prison to the clerk of the court'. Our complaint was that any such message was obviously intended to be conveyed to the relevant prison authorities and as it had not been conveyed to the prison there must have been a failure in the court system.

We had not been privy to the magistrates' private discussions at the court but by chance we had personal information which supported the statements in the inquiry report. I had spoken about our concerns one Sunday morning at the Anglican parish church and by coincidence one of the magistrates sitting at the time of Christopher's case had been in the congregation. Through Fr David Beeton she expressed a wish to meet us. It turned out that her three children had been confirmed into the Church of

England at the same ceremony as Christopher, so we had all been in contact before without any idea of the future tragedy which would bring us together again. We had no recollection of this. She gave us much the same description of events as was later contained in the inquiry report and sent a formal statement to the inquiry of her views.

Some months after we had submitted our complaint we were told it had been rejected. We were most astonished at the finding that the magistrates had not expressed any concern about Christopher's safety in prison and that therefore court officers could not be criticised for failing to pass any message to the prison. We sought a meeting with the two legal officers who had carried out the investigation in order to convey our grave doubts about the findings.

We arrived for the meeting which was held on Monday, 19 July 1999. One of them appeared to be very uneasy throughout the meeting and we were not reassured by their answers to our questions. Our notes of that meeting record that we were told by the investigating officers that all the magistrates and the clerk of the court had been questioned individually and the clerk had stated that she had not been informed of any concerns regarding Christopher nor had she been asked to convey those concerns to the prison. Furthermore she and two of the magistrates had stated they were not convinced of Christopher's mental illness. It was pointed out to us that these statements by the clerk of the court had been consistent throughout the investigation and also with the evidence she had given to the independent inquiry, as was clear from the transcript of her evidence which had been obtained. Notwithstanding this evidence, the inquiry report was absolutely clear in stating that the clerk of the court, the CPS officer and the duty solicitor 'all believed that Christopher Edwards required a psychiatric assessment and believed that there was a real possibility that he was acutely mentally ill. All three, together with the bench, considered whether Christopher Edwards could be remanded to hospital. It was concluded that there was no power to do so.'

All the evidence directly available to us supported the inquiry's conclusion. Paul had been asked in court whether he could provide details of Christopher's mental health; we had been asked in the court building to complete the form 'Remand for Medical Reports'; and been told by the court officers to find a psychiatric bed for Christopher. There was also the evidence of PC Astbury who had been in the courtroom and is quoted in the inquiry report as having telephoned Chelmsford Prison when he said that the magistrates had 'wanted to remand him [Christopher] to a mental hospital'. This had led to senior prison officers twice contacting the court to clarify whether he should be sent for hospital reports. We were now told that it had been decided no weight could be attached to the evidence of the magistrate to whom we had spoken.

We restated our doubts in a further letter to the officers who carried out the investigation and finally to the chairman of the MCC but to no avail. In the final official reponse, the MCC chairman indicated he had read all the papers and reviewed the methodology for the investigation and had

> . . . found the methodology sound and conclusions drawn from the investigations consistent with the evidence obtained . . . I have then considered the action taken by the justices' chief executive in review of the findings of the investigations and have found that this action was reasonable and unprejudiced . . . Having considered the facts most carefully I have reached the inescapable conclusion that the magistrates did not ask the legal adviser to pass any message to Chelmsford Prison and, more generally, that the legal adviser did not fail in any respect to meet the MCC's expectations of her.

The NHS Trust in considering our complaint stated that it could rely only on the inquiry report whereas we were told that the MCC complaints system was for conclusions to be based only on what was said to the investigating officer. The contrasting approaches had produced the same outcome—our complaint against professional staff was not upheld. [2]

•　　•　　•

In October 1998 we initiated a complaint to the Health and Safety Executive (H&SE) that Prison Service breaches of health and safety legislation had contributed to Christopher's death. On 30 April 2002 we were given a verbal summary of their findings. There had been systematic failures by the Prison Service; no risk assessment at reception; unsatisfactory health screening; poor standards of performance; inadequate training; a faulty cell alarm with suggestions of tampering and failure to report the alarm known to be faulty.

Action against an individual officer would fail because the officer could claim to be acting in accordance with prevailing practice at the time and not through malice or negligence. They could not take court action against the Prison Service or other public agencies because they enjoyed Crown immunity. A policy of Crown censure would be a waste of time because all it could produce would be a commitment to implement changes already introduced.

The H&SE did make clear that because of our formal complaint, which they had investigated in greater detail than usual, and reports by HM Chief Inspector of Prisons, it now took a closer interest in prisons and was developing liaison with the inspector. They were confident this would be maintained and strengthened. H&SE guidance on matters identified when investigating our complaint was being prepared.

At least some good had resulted from our complaint.

---

[2] The European Court (*Chapter 23*) adopted the 'extensive findings of fact' set out in the inquiry report to which neither party (i.e. including the UK Government: which presumably speaks for UK courts in such matters) objected.

CHAPTER 18

Operation Tilberg: The Investigation

At the end of the press conference for the release of the inquiry report, we had been introduced to the newly appointed assistant chief constable of Essex police, Mr Charles Clark (his predecessor, Mr Dickinson, having taken retirement). Mr Clark asked whether we would be interested in participating in a two-day conference on mentally disordered offenders, organized by the Home Office on behalf of the Norfolk, Suffolk and Essex Area Criminal Justice Liaison Committee, which was to take place in September. We readily agreed. As I was feeling very angry at the way things were developing, at the manner in which we had been treated generally, and at the long time it had taken for the agencies to accept that they had failed us, I said quite sharply that they 'would get the facts'. Then I departed rather abruptly. Not a good start for any future dialogue but reading the report and the subsequent press conference had been extremely stressful.

My anger was not diminished when later that day I saw the television coverage of interviews with the chief constable and the Deputy Director General of the Prison Service in which they both continued to deny any cover up. In our opinion they protested too much.

The conference took place in September at Dunston Hall Hotel and Country Club near Norwich and was very well attended by members of the judiciary, medical profession, legal profession, police and other people concerned with the criminal justice system. When the time approached on the first afternoon of the conference to deliver our presentation I felt extremely nervous. It was a dual presentation with myself relating Christopher's tragedy and Paul following with various recommendations. We did not pull our punches and were relieved to find that the presentation was well received.

At dinner we found ourselves sitting with Mr Clark and the head of the Essex Crown Prosecution Service (CPS). We grasped the opportunity to relate more details of our experiences with the police at the time of Christopher's death and, as a result, the next day Mr Clark advised us that he would instruct Detective Chief Inspector Macey to pay us a visit with a view to further clarification of the position. He also said he would consider referring the matter to the Police Complaints Authority (PCA). I could not help reflecting that the Essex police could have taken this action immediately after we had made similar remarks at the release of the inquiry report.

We had contacted the PCA ourselves in July 1995 with the intention of making a complaint that the Essex police had not, as we requested, extended their investigations into the possibility of criminal negligence by one or more of the public agencies; had failed to keep us informed; and had refused to release documentation to us. We were surprised to be told by the PCA that our complaint would have to be referred to the Essex police to see whether it could be accepted. In the event we chose not to proceed at that time as we assumed that the inquiry would investigate all our matters of concern. After publication of the inquiry report from which it was clear that not all of our matters of concern had been addressed we decided to proceed with our complaint.

True to his word, the deputy chief constable sent DCI Macey to see us. We did not know what the police would do but we had resolved to make our complaint, which we submitted to the PCA in November 1998. In it we set out our claim concerning the failings of the Essex police: prior to the tragedy; during the investigation; in their subsequent dealings with us; and in failing to fulfil their assurances of co-operation with the inquiry. Our central complaint was our allegation of collusion between police officers and the Prison Service to cover up what had happened in an attempt to protect their organizations from criticism.

Shortly after this complaint was submitted the PCA advised us that the Essex police had voluntarily referred the matter to them. A PCA member, Josephine Dobry, told us she would be supervising the investigation and that supervision by a PCA member happened only in a small proportion of the more serious cases. Arrangements began to be put in place to arrange a meeting between ourselves, Ms Dobry and a chief superintendent from the Suffolk police who was appointed to head the investigation. We then received a phone call from Ms Dobry advising us that she had withdrawn because she had personal ties with the Prison Service and she felt it would be inappropriate for her to continue as the Essex police relationship with the Prison Service was clearly a central part of our complaint.

This put us back to the beginning. Another member of the PCA, Alan Potts, took over supervision of the investigation and he chose superintendent Mark Gore from the Metropolitan police to head up the investigation. He was assisted by detective sergeant, Kevin Concannon who had an investigation background, and police sergeant Elaine Shackell, who had been working in complaints. It was arranged that Mr Potts and his whole team would visit us at home early in March 1999.

We waited for the team to arrive and eventually I spotted them walking towards the house: a group of five people, as Mr Potts had also invited his case worker, Andy Bonny. I thought they looked a very pleasant group and opened the door to be greeted by smiles all round. As each member entered the house they shook hands and introduced themselves. I remember joking that I felt like the Queen! The atmosphere was relaxed and we gathered round the dining table to discuss the issues.

Mr Potts was a lively personality who appeared to have the vigour to push the investigation along, whilst superintendent Gore was highly polished (and seemed rather young for his senior rank). Kevin Concannon came across as a quiet, thorough, decent detective but one who, on first impressions, was not likely to be influenced by inspiration or imagination; and Elaine Shackell was a no-nonsense, empathetic and determined person. It was a good introductory meeting: we got on well; readily provided additional information; and received assurances of determination to carry out a thorough and comprehensive investigation about which we would receive regular progress reports. I made it clear we were not seeking to 'crucify' the police; all we wanted was the complete truth on the public record. I asked how long they thought the investigation would take. Mr Potts stated that normally an investigation took about four months but because this was a more complex case he expected it would take about eight months. Elaine Shackell was to be the family liaison officer and she gave her personal assurance that she was very committed to our case.

This meeting was followed up by an invitation to visit the PCA office in central London to see how they operated and later the Metropolitan police base in north-west London. This included a visit to the police station at which Mark Gore was based. It gave us the opportunity to see in practice the implementation of a new police record form of prisoner details which had been introduced nationally as a result of Christopher's death and which was to accompany all people who are remanded to prison.

We were shown the cells (which put a chill through me); the medical room; the control room—which appeared to be a replica of the one in the TV programme *The Bill*—and various other offices. It was all quite fascinating. We were also provided with a pleasant lunch in the staff restaurant which we discovered was paid for by Essex police. It seems the costs of an investigation, other than the basic salary of the investigating officers, are charged up to the police force against which the complaint is made. While amused that the Essex police were in effect buying us lunch, we thought the budgeting process wrong—'He who pays the piper calls the tune'—and should certainly not apply to complaints against the police.

We were told all investigations were given a name and ours was 'Operation Tilberg'. This was simply the next name thrown out by the computer and had no significance in itself. Apparently in the past when police investigating teams had chosen the name for their own investigations they had tended to use names which had a double meaning, often causing embarrassment when referred to in court! The main burden of the investigation was carried out by sergeants Concannon and Shackell. We provided copies of documents when asked (and sometimes even if not asked!) and suggested the names of people we believed they should see; usually these suggestions were accepted. Sergeant Shackell, and occasionally DS Concannon, kept us informed of progress on a regular basis and we were quite satisfied with the way we were treated. They were patient with us when, anxious that they might overlook something, we kept making additional points.

Throughout much of the period of this investigation there was in the media ongoing criticism of the Metropolitan police as a consequence of the Stephen Lawrence case and the subsequent MacPherson report.[1] In our view, the Essex police treated us with less respect than the Lawrence family received and than we were now receiving from the Metropolitan police. It thus seemed perverse to us that it was the Metropolitan police who were receiving public criticism which the Essex police had escaped. The senior management of Essex police were at the time taking court action against some police officers because they had ill-treated police dogs, yet they had not disciplined any officers in relation to Christopher's tragedy. Despite being a great dog lover myself I could not help reflecting that it seemed the life of a dog was of greater importance to them than that of a young man.

•   •   •

Very early on I went through a lengthy statement with Sergeants Concannon and Shackell. This took up 22 pages with many more pages of attachments which were copies of key documents. Even then there were further points I had to make in subsequent statements. In all, this process took three days and was on occasions extremely painful and very draining. Paul and Clare also had to make statements.

The interchange of information and meetings continued and we were kept informed about developments. Various quite interesting pieces of information were relayed to us, although both police sergeants were very careful not to disclose the substance of their investigation. We learned that Governor Fowler, who had carried out the second internal investigation, had attached copies of the relevant police statements to her report. As her report and the statements attached made absolutely clear what had happened, it was impossible for us to accept the inquiry's suggestion of a misunderstanding. Not only was the report crystal clear and correct but it had attached to it the Essex police's own statements establishing the truth. We knew that Mr Sinclair, the Governor of Chelmsford Prison at the time, had died but we learned that his then deputy declined to see the PCA investigation team and that virtually all of the prison officers contacted by the PCA failed to respond to letters seeking a meeting. In addition all but one of the police officers concerned with the investigation—we think about 20—declined to answer questions during interview. We wondered why these officers kept silent. Was it because they knew they had been involved in a shameful experience but were not prepared to own up to it?

---

[1]   In which the Metropolitan police were found to suffer from institutional racism following failures in relation to the investigation of the murder of a black teenager.

We have never been able to discover who drafted the letter which the Director General of HM Prison Service sent to us and it was interesting to learn from the PCA investigation team that the Prison Service area manager has stated that he was not involved.

While the quality of our liaison with the Metropolitan police was excellent, both Paul and I sensed that at least one of the officers found it difficult to believe that police officers could be party to a cover-up after the event. We therefore again set out before them in writing all the factors supporting our allegations that there had been collusion between the police and the Prison Service to mislead us, though we acknowledged that such an agreement was not likely to be recorded in the minutes of a meeting, nor were any of those party to such an agreement likely to admit it now.

•   •   •

For some time I had felt a very strong compulsion to write a book about our experiences and this was compounded by various people, including DS Concannon, saying 'There ought to be a book about all this'. So by early 2000 I decided to have a go. In the course of going through our many files (over 20 in total) I came across a note made in 1995. This suggested that a lawyer connected with the case might be a useful source of information as to whether there had been a meeting between the police and Prison Service at which each initially blamed the other. We immediately passed this note to the investigating team and urged them to see this lawyer. We also wrote to a contact in that firm urging that the lawyer see the team. While another lawyer in the firm did so, the lawyer we had suggested, who had certainly been closely involved as he had been interviewed about the case on television, never made himself available for interview by the PCA team.

In April 2000 (17 months after lodging our complaint), we were told the Metropolitan police report of over 100 pages plus attachments had been formally handed to the PCA. They and the Metropolitan police would come separately to talk to us about it. Mr Potts came first and explained that the PCA procedures required the member who supervised the investigation to be replaced by another member, Mr Bynoe, who would vet the investigation report and conclusions and then be responsible for determining the disciplinary action to be taken.

Superintendent Gore and Sergeants Concannon and Shackell arrived at a later date and went through some points of the investigation with us. We learned from these meetings that a substantial number of our complaints had been upheld by the investigative team but it had been considered that there had not been sufficient evidence to establish beyond all reasonable doubt our allegation of collusion in a cover-up. The key decision, however, rested with the PCA and that would not be taken until after they had had an exchange of views with the Essex police. It was made clear to us that the

Metropolitan police investigation report could not be released to us because it was the property of Essex police. We later asked Essex police for a copy but it was refused.

At the end of the second meeting both Paul and I stated that though we disagreed with a number of conclusions they had reached, we appreciated the quality of the family liaison we had received from the investigative team. Supt Gore asked whether we would be prepared to put those remarks in writing, which we did happily a day or two later and sent them off.

•   •   •

After the departure of the team Paul and I took our daily walk, which included a visit to Christopher's grave, and were astonished and very touched to find a lovely bouquet placed there by the three police officers. I have kept the accompanying card with its Christian message in the book containing the hundreds of letters of consolation we have received, together with three flowers from the bouquet which I dried and pressed.

CHAPTER 19

Operation Tilberg: The Outcome

Mr Bynoe took over the PCA investigation at the end of July 2000 and he advised us that in view of the complex issues it would take some weeks to reach a conclusion. In early October he told us that he expected a conclusion 'within about three weeks.' Time stretched out and as we had not heard from the PCA we tried to contact Mr Bynoe but for a long period could not get through to him. Eventually, however, contact was made. I recall that I had a telephone conversation with Mr Bynoe in which he said it was taking time as he tried to be fair to both parties. We felt it was not a question of being fair to both parties; it was a question purely of establishing the facts and thereby the truth.

It was not until December 15 that Mr Bynoe wrote us a formal letter consisting of 24 pages setting out in detail the conclusions reached by the PCA. The majority of our complaints were upheld, including those about:

- failures in the treatment of Christopher by not calling in the police surgeon and not filling in the Form CID2;[1]
- several failures in the investigation process, including critically the failure to widen the investigation in spite of repeated requests to do so including a written request to which no reply had been received;
- failures in family liaison after the tragedy, including being told over the phone that Christopher had been murdered;[2] not being seen by the investigating police officer until ten days after the tragedy; and learning in court that Christopher's ear was missing.

Most of the complaints not upheld were those of least significance to us, but there were some which were of greater import. The most important was the failure to uphold our allegation of collusion. We had been told that the standard of proof required for our complaint was 'beyond all reasonable doubt' (though this standard has been reduced for later complainants to 'the balance of probabilities') and we had recognised that in the absence of documentary evidence or a personal confession this would be hard to achieve. We had, however, expected the PCA report to lay out in an even handed way the arguments for and against collusion and

---

[1]   The form then used by Essex police to advise a prison governor of a prisoner who presented a special risk, including mental disturbance or an extremely violent nature (see the inquiry report at p.352).
[2]   As explained in earlier chapters, although an officer called at our home on the very first day, the reason for Christopher's death was relayed by telephone.

then to conclude that by the very severe standards it was required to apply it was unable to uphold our complaint.

But the PCA did not do this. It had concluded that a lack of communication and co-operation between the Essex police and the Prison Service had created a perception or 'illusion' of collusion. This was contrary to the police inspector's own statement to the investigation team that there had been regular contact with the prison, which Paul had recorded in a note of a phone call from Kevin Concannon. I ruefully observed that it was ironic that the inquiry report should have decided that there had been no collusion between the Essex police and the Prison Service, only a misunderstanding in communication; while the PCA had decided the evidence pointed to a lack of communication and co-operation between the two agencies and therefore no collusion.

•   •   •

Mr Bynoe arranged to see us, accompanied by his case worker, on January 3 to go over the PCA findings. We went through his letter carefully with most emphasis on our allegation of a cover up. We pointed out that if the inspector had, as he claimed, told us that the two young men had not met until placed in the same cell this would have contradicted the statement in the letter we received from the Prison Service (within a day of meeting the inspector) in which it was stated the two had met in reception, got on well and asked not to be separated. If this had happened we would have immediately challenged two different explanations (given within a day of each other) of the same critical event. It was inconceivable, we said, that any family desperately seeking the truth about the death of their son would fail to challenge two contradictory explanations of what happened.

The PCA did not offer any explanation of this but claimed there were two key factors tending to undermine the case for collusion. The first was based on the fact that in separate statements to the press on the morning of the homicide the police superintendent and Governor Sinclair stated that the two young men had not met until they were placed in the same cell. The PCA said it was unlikely in view of these statements that the two organizations would later change their story about where they had met.

We pointed out that the PCA argument was completely untenable because it was on the record that a few days after telling the media the two had not met until placed in the same cell Governor Sinclair wrote and told us the two had first met in the prison reception. If the Prison Service had changed its story so quickly why should not the police? Indeed, if the police had not changed their explanation to match that of Governor Sinclair we would have received contradictory explanations—which we would have challenged. The acknowledged fact that the two agencies were telling us the same story ten days after telling the media a different one was, we maintained, strong argument supporting our allegation of collusion.[3]

We then turned to the second key point the PCA claimed undermined the case for collusion: namely that while our notes of early meetings had certainly queried the suggestion that Richard and Christopher had formed a friendly relationship we had not queried that they had met in prison reception. We pointed out that we knew from the outset that Christopher's personality and mental health would make it highly improbable he would strike up a friendship and therefore we questioned that suggestion. We were not in a position to challenge the assertion that the two had met in prison reception until August 1995 when we learned the true facts from the copies of the police statements which had been sent to us.

We made all these points and more to Mr Bynoe. He made it clear that he wished only to note them but he would study them in the light of the evidence on the file and then respond more fully. We recollect Mr Bynoe stating that our case had to meet the criterion of 'beyond reasonable doubt' which prevailed at the time, rather than the lesser standard of 'a balance of probabilities' which now applies.

We accepted his statement that he would consider our observations and within a few days of the meeting we sent him a letter setting out our criticisms of his initial findings and then awaited the outcome. We had some time to wait.

There had been a curious moment while Mr Bynoe was meeting with us at our home. The phone rang and I answered it and came back to Paul and Mr Bynoe sitting in the next room and told Paul (I hope in a slightly conspiratorial way) that the *Daily Telegraph* was on the phone for him and I suggested he take the call upstairs. This was perfectly true, however it had nothing to do with our case but with an issue relating to possible Government changes to national insurance arrangements for people who had spent time in Australia, about which Paul had previously been in touch with one of the financial journalists! I very much hoped, however, that Mr Bynoe would assume it was in connection with our case.

---

[3] Readers may have noted from other parts of the book the occasional laxity in official accounts with regard to dates and events.

We were told that *Private Eye* did contact the PCA because they were preparing an article which linked the misleading information given to us by the Prison Service with a House of Commons Select Committee report that had been very critical of the Prison Service for the provision of misleading information about an internally organized raid on Blantyre House Prison which the committee thought was totally unjustified.

A few days after Mr Bynoe's visit we attended a conference on 'Deaths in Custody' at Reading University. A PCA speaker was listed on the programme but the person who turned up was not as named in the programme but chairman, Sir Alistair Graham. We had found at other conferences that people of his distinction were usually carefully shepherded by the conference organizers but at the morning coffee break we noticed Sir Alistair standing on his own. So we buttonholed him, introduced ourselves, expressed our concern that we felt the PCA judgement in our case contained some serious errors and asked him what could be done about it. He spoke highly of Mr Bynoe and undertook to raise the matter with him.

•   •   •

The PCA reply when it eventually came in early March was very unsatisfactory. The letter totally ignored two of our key criticisms: their conclusion that the Prison Service and Essex police would not later contradict their initial public statements was undermined by the fact the Prison Service manifestly had done so; and it was implausible to assume that a bereaved family in search of the truth would accept without challenge two different explanations of what happened given by two public agencies within the space of 24 hours.

For the remainder, the reaction to the points we had made was to use the investigation report in what seemed to us an arbitrary, selective and inconsistent way to support their original determination. The PCA would still not even accept that a four-year delay in implementing the Home Office 1990 circular[1] showed that Essex police had been dilatory.

It appeared to us that the PCA had negotiated some agreement with the Essex police during the nine months between receipt of the investigation report and the formal response to us, and the PCA was not prepared to modify its original decision in any way. This view was strengthened some months later when, going through the papers again, we noted that the text of the PCA official statement on the outcome of the investigation clearly stated that 'the following 15 allegations have been substantiated by the investigation' but it then only listed 12. Maybe the PCA officers have shaky arithmetic but we thought it more likely that they had originally upheld 15 of our allegations but had been persuaded out of

---

[1]   HOC 66/90 'Provision for Mentally Disordered Offenders'.

three of them in consultation with the Essex police and had overlooked the necessary changes to an already prepared statement.

We realised that the PCA had fixed its position, however shaky that might be, and it would be pointless to try and obtain any change by further direct contact with them. We thought it probable that we had sufficient evidence to ensure their decision would be overturned if we sought a judicial review in the High Court but we did not have the financial resources to initiate such an action. We had become aware that the Government planned to make substantial changes to the PCA and its processes to try and increase public confidence and trust in the police and in the complaints system and concluded those changes were long overdue.

There were several other points in the PCA letter which reinforced our conviction of the inadequate nature of the report of the multi-agency inquiry. The investigating team had contacted the inquiry secretariat asking about the background to the paragraph in the report suggesting that the police believed Christopher and Richard met in the reception area as a result of what they had been told by the Prison Service, which the PCA said was clearly wrong. Mrs Kent had responded on behalf of the secretariat and told the investigating team that 'she was unable to clarify the situation'; 'she had no knowledge as to who wrote that particular paragraph and was not responsible for checking the factual accuracy of the draft report.' She suggested that the head of legal services of Essex County Council might be able to assist. When contacted he was 'unable to assist as to whether an error existed and if so how it came to be made within the report'. It brought to mind a clear recollection that the investigating team had told us that they had written on the same subject to the inquiry chairman, who had stated in the report that the matter had been looked into carefully, but the team told us that they had—at least at that stage—not received any reply.

•   •   •

The final stage was the public release of the PCA report which produced a flurry of activity. The local press covered the issues extensively as did *The Guardian* and *The Times*. Paul and I were interviewed on the radio and both the BBC and ITV sent a TV crew to interview us. Each wanted to film us by Christopher's grave and in one item I must have appeared under great stress trying to control my emotions. Though true, the main reason for my appearance was that I was freezing cold and trying to stop my teeth from chattering! We learned from friends that we had been seen and heard in London and the north-east of England. We were glad that the failures of the Essex police were being given wide publicity, which forced public reassurances of better performance. We also received a letter of apology from the chief constable and an offer to meet with us which we readily accepted. We later had three meetings with him although we were unable to reach agreement. He initially appeared to wish to put Restorative

Justice principles into practice by seeking reconciliation with us. When the discussion turned to the question of some reparation to us, however, he was obviously constrained by his legal advisers and eventually he suspended discussion until after the European Court of Human Rights, to which we were in the process of taking our case (see *Chapter 23*), had announced its decision. Following that decision he wrote to say he did not feel it would be appropriate to enter into further discussions and that he did not feel a further meeting would be beneficial.

● ● ●

An interesting footnote to our PCA complaint emerged early in 2002. After the press coverage of the PCA report a former employee of the Essex police wrote to the PCA in April 2001 stating that one of his former colleagues (who had previously been a prison officer) had told him at the time that Christopher's mental condition had been recognised and that he was deliberately required to share a cell with another unstable prisoner. A further investigation was then made jointly by the Essex police and the Metropolitan police but the other people involved disputed the allegations made about them and the police advised us that the matter could not be taken further.

CHAPTER 20

Liberty

Our first contact with the civil rights organization Liberty came through a recommendation from Anita Dockley of the Howard League, whom we had briefed in anticipation of the release of the inquiry report in 1997.

Paul then met John Wadham, the director of Liberty, at a conference in 1997 organized by the Institute for the Study and Treatment of Delinquency[1] at which we conducted a workshop on our experience. He agreed in principle that Liberty would consider taking Christopher's case to the European Court of Human Rights (ECHR) but said that a final decision could not be made until the report of the inquiry was published. We contacted Liberty again after the report was available and provided them with a copy and copious other documentation.

Philip Leach, who was the Liberty solicitor mainly concerned with our case at the outset, proved to be a quiet, dedicated and sympathetic source of support. He agreed there was a strong case to be made that various rights had been infringed, particularly Christopher's right to life. We met later in chambers with Philip Leach and Murray Hunt, a barrister experienced in human rights law, who had been appointed by Liberty to present our case to the ECHR. Murray Hunt was considerate, understanding and impressed us far more than any of the other barristers we had met because of his sharp mind, ability to communicate and genuine human sympathy. We felt our case was in good hands.

Our role was to provide the basic factual information so that Philip and Murray could identify how what had happened contravened the provisions of the European Convention on Human Rights. In summary the Liberty application on our behalf argued that four articles of the Convention had been breached:

- Christopher had been denied his right to life under Article 2;
- we had been denied effective access to court to bring civil proceedings under Article 6(1);
- the lack of a right of access to court coupled with the lack of any other independent investigative mechanism was a failure to respect family life thus breaching Article 8;
- Article 13 had been breached because we did not have an effective remedy in national law for an independent adjudication of our claim; and

---

[1] Now the Centre for Crime and Justice Studies.

- the authorities had not done all they could to protect Christopher's life, or to enable us to obtain redress.

We were warned that the case would take a long time because of the delays implicit in the European court system and the volume of cases being submitted to it. In some ways the process appeared like an obstacle race but happily, guided by Liberty's expert handling, our application survived every hurdle and went forward for judgement.

Our application had to be made against the UK Government and sustained against their counter-arguments. It drove home to us that whereas we were brought up to believe the Government was the impartial external body ensuring fairness in dealings between individuals and organizations, with particular emphasis on supporting the small and weak against the big and strong, this was not the case when the big and strong was an agency of government itself. In these cases—such as ours—the Government seeks with public funds to defend the public agencies—in this case the Prison Service and Essex police—against individuals such as ourselves. We really now appreciate the merit of having a European Court to which these kinds of cases can be taken.

Nor were the government lawyers scrupulous in the arguments they used. We were—perhaps naively—shocked when we saw that in one of their counterclaims the government lawyer stated, 'The authorities at Chelmsford Prison were not formally warned that [Richard Linford] was dangerous probably because the level of dangerousness was not considered exceptional.' This statement was made despite the fact it had been acknowledged by all the government agencies that a formal warning should have been given to the prison by the police but had not been because of inadequacies in training and in the form involved. It was government recognition of the failure to give proper notice of the acknowledged dangerous nature of Richard Linford that led to the decision to introduce a new prisoner escort record form throughout the country, to try and ensure such a failure was not repeated.

Another example of the lack of integrity of the government submissions to the ECHR was the argument that while it was regrettable that the cell call button was not functioning properly, no system could rule out the possibility of mechanical defects. This was despite a clear statement in the inquiry report, obviously based on official records: 'We were also told that there were no known mechanical defects in the system at the time of Christopher Edwards death'. The strong implication in the inquiry report is that the buzzer system had been tampered with from outside the cell.

During the course of our several years dealing with lawyers as a result of the case we had formed a very low opinion of legal professionals in general. That was never true of the lawyers we met at or through Liberty:

John Wadham, Murray Hunt, Philip Leach, who was succeeded by Chitra Karve and she in turn by Nancy Collins assisted by a trainee, Rosalind Drysdale. They were all able, sympathetic, keen to communicate and very committed. We were always kept fully informed down to the smallest detail and our welfare was always taken into consideration. We very much appreciated too that we were receiving this excellent service free of charge, for we could never have afforded the substantial costs involved in bringing a case to the ECHR. We were happy to agree to details of Christopher's case being used by Liberty in a Christmas appeal letter in December 1998 and while we understand this raised some thousands of pounds the funds would still have fallen well short of the full costs involved.

The process of working with Liberty was constructive and liberating for us. Our and their prime concern was to secure a positive judgement from the European Court and for this reason we had no hesitation in turning down the UK government's offer of a £20,000 out of court settlement. We embarked on the case to secure a decision from the ECHR which would clearly identify the various breaches of human rights which Christopher and we had suffered in order to try and ensure both justice for Christopher and that such denials of human rights did not occur again. The value of a positive decision by the ECHR would far outweigh any monetary compensation. It was hurtful to be given the message that in the eyes of the government the death of our beloved son while in the care of a government agency, and the anguish his death brought us, were considered to merit much less compensation than the levels of award which, according to press reports, were routinely made to police officers who sustained an injury while carrying out their duties.

•   •   •

The examples of misrepresentation in the Government's case which we had encountered brought home to us that this was not government for the people, it was government for the public institutions at the expense of the people. As such, we believe it to be contrary to the very spirit of human rights legislation and the jurisprudence of the European Court: under which a positive duty is cast on states to actively promote and protect the rights of citizens. Whatever may be the rhetoric, the United Kingdom has—as many individuals needing to deal with public institutions in this country will have discovered—a long way to go before it can be said that it is adopting a meaningful approach to its responsibilities rather than a defensive one. As will be seen from *Chapter 23* we have every reason to value the fact that we were able, ultimately, to resort to Europe in defence of our—and Christopher's—fundamental rights.

CHAPTER 21

Progress with the Agencies

As relations with the agencies improved, there was in a number of cases a mutual wish to work together. An early illustration, while the inquiry was still proceeding, was a request from the Prison Service representative, Martin McHugh, to set out our experiences of dealing with the service after the tragedy, so that they could take it into account in devising new policies for relationships with families bereaved by a death in custody. At a later stage we were provided with a draft of the proposed new policy, then the final version. It was encouraging to realise that HM Prison Service implicitly acknowledged that the way we had been treated was unacceptable and wished to set new and better standards for the future.

As described in earlier chapters, we had previously established contact with the then Chief Inspector of Prisons, General Sir David Ramsbotham, and we had sent him a copy of our interim reflections on the inquiry. He was most appreciative—particularly because of the sections relating to the proper treatment of bereaved families—as he had already recognised from other experiences that there was a need to improve significantly relationships with all families bereaved by a death in custody.

We knew that Richard Linford's case would be reviewed periodically by a mental health tribunal with a view to determining when he would be released into the community. We wrote to the tribunal to ask if we could be informed when Richard's case would be heard and the date by when any submission had to be lodged. After some time the tribunal responded to say that the arrangements were under review and our letter had been referred to the Department of Health for it to answer. Some time later the department advised us we would be told in due course what the new arrangements were.

We bear no ill will towards Richard as he, like Christopher, was failed by the health and criminal justice systems. It is clear from his history that he is—or was—potentially a very dangerous person and that he will probably always require some form of medical supervision. Moreover, as his mother has told us, he is now receiving better treatment than he had before the tragedy and is probably more content with his life.

When the mental health professionals do, however, consider the question of release we believe that the victim's family should be consulted. We would want to make the argument that in the light of his previous history Richard should not be released until it can be guaranteed that he will continue to receive and accept his medication while in the community. In our view the occasion of his release should create the opportunity to put a binding obligation on the mental health services to ensure they do their job properly in future, particularly as they failed so dismally in the past.

We would also wish that a condition of release should be that Richard would make no attempt to contact us, for while we bore him no ill will we could not accept the prospect of meeting face-to-face the live young man who had taken the life of Christopher. Other people bereaved by homicide by a paranoid schizophrenic have told us of their fears of being confronted by the person who destroyed their loved one. In April 2002 we were given the opportunity of conveying our views to the team responsible for his welfare and were assured that they would be taken into account.

•   •   •

Some time after the release of the inquiry report, the commissioning agents invited us to a meeting to discuss what would happen next. They took the view that a video could be a useful inter-agency training tool and it was agreed there should be a further meeting to discuss the project in more detail. The matter of a memorial to Christopher was raised and the commissioning agents suggested the most appropriate memorial would be a bursary in Christopher's name. My immediate reaction was not one of enthusiasm but Paul and I agreed to think it over and make a decision at a later date. In the event, we wrote and thanked the commissioning agents for their offer of a bursary but while we wished the project every success we did not wish Christopher's name to be associated with it. We thought it would be more appropriate if one of the new mental health units which were planned was named after Christopher as a visible and lasting tribute. However we accepted the commissioning agencies' subsequent advice that they were not prepared to agree to this proposal and dismissed the matter from our minds.

In December 1998 we attended a meeting at Essex police headquarters to discuss an inter-agency training video. Those present were: the police training officer and representatives from the Prison Service Training Department; social services; health professionals and the Essex police video crew. There was much discussion about how to proceed and it was left that the agencies would co-operate in the preparation of a suitable outline. We were shown around the video suite by the crew and were most impressed by the unit's professionalism and equipment, which seemed very up-to-date. In the event we heard nothing further! One positive result of the meeting was that the training officer seemed quite interested in using our experience and we have since on two or three occasions spoken to newly qualified custody sergeants, which I hope has proved useful.

Early in June 1999 we were greatly surprised to receive a letter from the Mid-Essex Health Trust advising us that it had reconsidered its earlier decision and suggesting that it name a proposed psychiatric intensive care unit, which was to be created as soon as planning permission was received, in memory of Christopher. We had a further meeting with the trust to view the plans and were delighted to agree to the naming of the new unit in Christopher's memory. In July 2000 we attended the official 'turning the first sod' ceremony and retain amusing photographs of ourselves and the chairman of the trust wearing hard hats.

Early in 2001 a new mental health trust was formed by amalgamation of previous trusts and the incorporation of the local authority mental health services team. We were invited to attend the handing over of the keys of the centre to the new chairman, Mary St Aubyn, and were received in a very warm and supportive manner. We had thought some national figure would be invited to perform the opening ceremony but in the event we were asked to do so.

It was a very moving moment when, on 2 July 2001, we arrived at the hospital site and saw the signs indicating the direction to The Christopher Unit. In my brief remarks I emphasised how appreciative we were, firstly that Christopher's name would be permanently associated with a much needed new service to help those suffering a crisis in their mental illness and, secondly, of the generosity of spirit shown by the NHS trust both in naming the unit after Christopher and inviting us to open it.

•   •   •

Enter Ivor Ward the new area manager for the prisons in East Anglia whom we first met at the Norwich criminal justice conference organized by the Home Office. As we got to know him better we realised that here was one senior manager in the Prison Service really dedicated to the proper care of prisoners and their families. He dealt with the difficult subject of sending the mentally ill to prison with warmth and humanity. Ivor broached the idea with us of making a training video independent of the other agencies and we said we would be prepared to do that as we were anxious to help in any way we could. He followed this up with an invitation to go to HM Prison Highpoint to talk to the governors of all the prisons in his area, along with one or two specialist advisers.

March 1999 saw us arriving at Highpoint for the meeting, to be warmly greeted by Alison Gomme, the new Governor of Chelmsford Prison, whom we had already met when she had visited us at home to assure us of her sympathy and support. We made our presentation to the assembled prison Governors. It seemed to go quite well and was followed by a constructive discussion with those present.

As the idea was proving worthwhile in practice, Ivor invited us to visit Highpoint again to make a similar presentation to other staff. This was video-taped by one of the prison staff. Shortly afterwards we received a working copy. It was then decided to go ahead with a final version using the facilities at the Prison Service College at Newbold Revel.

First of all we were invited to meet the video crew to obtain some insight into the technology and familiarise ourselves with the surroundings. We were well looked after and enjoyed a homely lunch in the presence of prison officers and Governors. We made our second visit to Newbold Revel in November 1999 when the final version of the video was filmed and it was then available for use in training staff how to deal with mentally disordered offenders and how to relate to bereaved relatives.

One day Ivor Ward sent us a copy of *Prison Service Journal* in which Mike Jenkins, the Prison Service nominee on the inquiry panel, had written an article about Christopher's tragedy which acknowledged some of the errors but resolutely denied any idea of a cover-up. We immediately wrote to the editor a letter which was published in a later issue contrasting Mr Jenkins' confident assurance with the Parliamentary Ombudsman's statement that he 'found fully justified the complaint by Mr and Mrs Edwards that the Prison Service had misled them as to some of the circumstances which had led to the death in custody of their son'!

We maintained contact with Ivor Ward and Alison Gomme who generously suggested that a new garden-cum-play area for children just outside the wall of Chelmsford Prison be associated with Christopher as a memorial. We were very touched by this suggestion and after further discussion with Alison and the prison chaplain, Canon Geoffrey Hayward, we suggested the area be named after Christopher and there be a plaque bearing his name and an appropriate message, which was readily agreed.

It took a while to bring the idea into reality but eventually it was formally opened on 27 March 2001 by the Minister for Prisons, Paul Boateng, with the MP for Chelmsford, Simon Burns, in attendance. Unfortunately due to a misunderstanding between myself and the Governor's secretary I had thought we were expected to arrive at about 4.00 p.m. Paul Boateng was, however, expecting to see us at approximately 3.00 p.m. for about 30 minutes before he formally opened the garden. We did not get to the prison in time to meet him but he did kindly ring and speak to us on the telephone.

Although we arrived too late to meet the minister and his Parliamentary colleagues, this mishap did not prevent us from appreciating the very attractive garden with its plaque in memory of Christopher bearing the quotation from Matthew, Chapter XXV: 'I was in prison and you visited me.' It was good to receive a warm welcome from the Prison Service staff, the Board of Visitors and the volunteers at the prison visitors' centre. The volunteers had put a lot of work into planning and organizing the garden and we much appreciated their readiness to associate it with Christopher. For us, it became linked to the measures being taken by Martin Narey, the new Director General, to try to improve prison culture, part of a process of reconciliation and healing.

We had first met Martin Narey at the annual conference of Unlock, the National Association of Ex-Offenders. Early in 2000, Ivor Ward invited us to have a 'cup of tea' with Mr Narey. We were naturally delighted to accept and duly turned up at Prison Service headquarters, where we took a seat in reception to await Mr Narey's secretary. We were utterly taken aback to see Mr Narey himself emerge from the lift to greet us and escort us to his office. On all the occasions we had had meetings with various dignitaries and heads of organizations, including on previous occasions when we had met with earlier Directors General of the Prison Service, we had never been shown such courtesy.

As the talks with Mr Narey and some of his staff, which had been conducted in a friendly manner, were drawing to a close Paul told them of the plan we had formulated on behalf of various Christian groups to distribute supportive leaflets throughout the churches and faith communities in Essex during Prisons Week in November. He asked whether the Prison Service could suggest a charitable body interested in penal issues which might be prepared to make a donation towards the cost of the leaflets. To our surprise Mr Narey immediately said the Prison Service would be prepared to print the leaflets and when Paul suggested 100,000 he did not demur.

On leaving the building, Paul and I reflected how impressed we had been with Martin Narey as a person of real integrity rather than superficial charm. As with Ivor Ward, his dedication was apparent. We felt that perhaps at last the Prison Service had an opportunity of being steered in the right direction even though that direction might be uphill all the way. It was clear now that there was a group of key people within the Prison Service who recognised a duty of care to prisoners and their families; who were keen to improve regimes within prisons; and to enable those leaving prison to lead a worthwhile life without re-offending.

Our opinion was confirmed later when we were able to compare the treatment of the family of Zahid Mubarek, who was beaten to death by his cellmate in Feltham Young Offenders' Institution, with the treatment we had received in comparable circumstances. The Prison Service made no effort to contact us and when we approached them we got a 'hands-off' response; little information was given to us and key parts of it were subsequently acknowledged to be untrue. By contrast, Martin Narey wrote to the family in very sympathetic terms within a few days of the tragedy and acknowledged the Prison Service's failure to discharge its proper responsibilities. We understand that the family gained some comfort from this empathetic approach.

CHAPTER 22

Progress with the Community

We had initially been concerned to establish the truth of Christopher's death for our own sake and so that the institutions could learn from the experience. Gradually we were realising that we might be able to make a contribution to a wider debate in the community. We knew from our own experience that coping with a member of the family who suffers mental illness is emotionally and physically draining and that when this is followed by a sudden death—including by suicide or homicide—the impact can be devastating, leaving a family totally stunned. We felt it important that this experience be shared with ordinary people as well as with the professionals and agencies involved so that community support could help bring about the needed changes.

An early opportunity arose when a group called Victims' Voice invited us to participate in a presentation to MPs in the House of Commons. A number of families told of their tragedies of losing a family member through violence by someone who was mentally ill. Each story was horrifying in its own way and we could only hope that those MPs who were present appreciated the need for new policies for the mentally ill, especially those who offend.

By 1997 I had become convinced that we needed to try to inform the community if real changes in the treatment of mentally ill people and offenders were to be implemented. Paul had always been more sceptical about such an approach but we kept turning the issue over in our mind. Early in that year the Catholic Bishops had issued a document, *The Common Good*, which emphasised the responsibility of individual Christians to work for the good of others. As a result Paul was involved in organizing a meeting at his local church addressed by a voluntary agency which provided retraining for the unemployed and also recycled computer equipment for use in the Third World. This initiative led us to suggest to Father Arthur, the parish priest, that we might talk at a similar meeting.

The meeting which had been promoted in each of the local churches took place in the church meeting room in January 1998 and there was a good attendance. By this time the Government had announced its intention to consider major changes to the Care in the Community policy and almost as an afterthought we decided to prepare and take to the meeting a petition to request the Prime Minister to ensure action was taken to:

(a) increase substantially and quickly the supply of secure psychiatric beds;

(b) change mental health law and practice so that mentally ill people unaware of their illness are not denied hospitalisation or medication because they do not ask for it;

(c) cease sending mentally ill people to prison (where official surveys show they represent 66 per cent of remand prisoners and 39 per cent of sentenced prisoners) thereby releasing capital funds for the planned new secure psychiatric beds; and

(d) insist that all criminal justice and mental health agencies demonstrate a consistent high standard duty of care to the mentally ill people for whom they have responsibility.

At the meeting we outlined Christopher's tragedy and subsequent events and how it had led us to recognise the national scandal of sending thousands of mentally ill people to prison and our conviction that for the common good we are all challenged to change this social evil. The presentation went well and the petition was well supported. Fr. Arthur agreed we could collect signatures from people who had not been able to attend the meeting by standing outside church after each of the three Sunday services. The petition then took on a life of its own. The ministers of the other Christian churches in Coggeshall readily agreed that we could speak at their churches so I spoke at the Anglican Church and Paul at the local United Free Church. On each occasion we received warm support and the number of signatures rose to several hundred.

People who had heard us speak asked if they could have copies of the petition form so they could collect signatures from friends or work colleagues. In view of their genuine interest we thought we might promote the initiative more widely ourselves and so we wrote to family members and friends in different parts of the country inviting their support. We never encountered any difficulty in securing signatures to the petition. As soon as people learned the facts they wanted to sign and in many cases to go out and seek signatures themselves. Our local newsagent offered to make the petition available for signature in his shop and he very soon collected over 100 signatures.

We became more ambitious in our attempts to secure signatures. The editor of the local church newspaper agreed to carry an article together with a petition form and we also contacted *The Tablet*, the national Catholic magazine. It was willing to carry a story and include a petition form as an advertisement, but not in the same issue. Our contact with *The Tablet* was the advertisement manager, Conor Taaffe, who we discovered had been the first person to come to the assistance of Stephen Lawrence as he lay dying on a street in Eltham. The unfolding of the tragedy of Stephen Lawrence and its aftermath was a continuing backdrop to our own tragedy.

We also very much empathised with the Lawrence family. We, like them, had lost a loved and talented son; the police investigations in both cases had been criticised and were questionable; and the individuals primarily responsible for both tragedies had escaped what we believed were their just deserts. Richard Linford had been sentenced but those whose actions or failures led to the two young men ending up in the same cell had, at various points in the process, escaped any form of censure. The Lawrence family might be surprised at how we envied them. They had well meaning if ineffectual police liaison on a daily basis immediately after the tragedy. We did not see a police officer involved with the investigation for ten days. In contrast to our position, they seemed to have plenty of legal resources plus the high-powered support of the national media. The MacPherson report has been criticised on the grounds that it was programmed to find in favour of the Lawrence family's complaint, whereas our inquiry—in our view—served to minimise the failures of the public agencies and individuals involved.

The reason why our two families were treated differently is, we believe, the same reason why penal reform organizations give a higher priority to issues relating to the position of women prisoners although they are much smaller in numbers than mentally ill prisoners. There is a significant number of members of the black community and ethnic minorities and women engaged in social action. They have a loyalty to oppressed members of their group and are ready to fight for them through powerful black and feminist lobbies against the white male dominated public institutions which, they perceive, have been the cause of oppression of black people, ethnic minorities and women. There is not the same degree of active community support for the mentally ill. Those who know most about the issues are either mentally ill themselves and inhibited by their condition from fighting for their fellow sufferers, or carers who are exhausted and drained by their responsibilities and do not have the time or the mental energy to fight campaigns on the same scale. We certainly did not experience white male dominated institutions protecting their own kind—like Christopher—at the expense of members of ethnic minorities and women. They were only concerned with protecting themselves as institutions.

The same phenomenon was evident much later following the tragic homicide in Feltham YOI mentioned in *Chapter 21* where a prisoner beat his cellmate, Zahid Mubarek, to death. There were obvious parallels with Christopher's tragedy though one major difference was that the Prison Service was quick to acknowledge its own failures and to make available copies of the internal investigation report.

A few days later a white prisoner in Cardiff Prison, Colin Bloomfield, was killed and disembowelled. The national reaction to both tragedies demonstrated the influence of the strong lobbies against racial discrimination. There was virtually no national coverage of the

Bloomfield case, which on objective evidence was no less shocking than that of Zahid Mubarek, while that case attracted national publicity in the media, including the Director General of the Prison Service making a public apology.

We have met many members of the black and ethnic minority communities who are wholly convinced that unnatural deaths in custody are predominantly among members of their communities. This belief has led them to a conviction that society is irredeemably racist. Yet on the figures available to us such deaths occur primarily among the white community. According to a list in the authoritative *The Prisons Handbook,* non-white people accounted for 12 per cent of the 101 self-inflicted deaths in prison between July 1999 and July 2000, while figures published by the Home Office show that during the same period non-white prisoners represented 19 per cent of the total prison population. There were only two homicides in prison during that period—the cases of Zahid Mubarek and Colin Bloomfield to which I have already referred. While racial discrimination is an evil which should be exposed and eliminated, it would be unfortunate if factors common to the tragedies of Christopher, Zahid Mubarek and Colin Bloomfield—such as the sending of severely psychotic individuals to prison rather than secure hospitals; inadequate Prison Service risk assessment processes; inappropriate cell allocation; and poor management of vulnerable prisoners—were not given at least the same degree of attention and action as racism.

Returning to the story of the petition, the Anglican Diocese of Chelmsford, responding to our approach, supplied 700 plus labels with addresses so we could write to all the churches in the diocese inviting support for the petition. The flow of completed petition forms now came in on a daily basis and we looked forward to the sound of the mail dropping through our letterbox each day. The number of signatures crept up into the thousands to reach levels we did not even dream about at the outset. Through this outreach we not only obtained signatures, we also received hundreds of messages of support which were heart-warming and often caused us to be moved to tears. But we knew we were right in what we were doing. As one letter put it, 'In many ways the campaign you have initiated will keep the wound wider and less healed than it would otherwise become if you quietly closed the door of your mind on it. Yet God sometimes calls us to the steep and rugged pathways so that good can triumph'.

We were deeply touched by the real practical sympathy of so many people who were prepared to go out and obtain signatures for the petition—occasionally running into hundreds—from their local communities. One of these was a dynamic Scot, Margaret Paton, who had fought and overcome many obstacles to rescue her daughter from the difficulties caused by her mental illness. In addition to caring for her daughter she had also formed a very active carers' group in Ayr. She invited us to speak to them and also to a journalist from a Glasgow newspaper.

We received very strong support from both the group and the newspaper and recognised again that the greatest knowledge of the practical consequences of mental illness and the greatest commitment to overcoming them is to be found in carers, whose views are often ignored by professionals. The too frequent disparagement of carers was illustrated in a letter from the secretary of one parish council returning the signed petition forms. His wife had been severely mentally ill to the extent she had threatened his life before taking her own. 'The worst aspect', he wrote, 'is a complete lack of understanding and support not just from society as a whole but from the professionals.' Margaret Paton's dynamism and dedication made sure that would not happen in Ayrshire. At a later stage we were pleased to support her when Paul spoke at a rally she had organized in Princes Street Gardens in Edinburgh.

During all this time we received support from the local Braintree Carers' Group, comprising mainly parents of adult children who were suffering mental illness. Some had endured many years of sustained stress caring for their loved ones and not always with positive or sympathetic support from the responsible agencies. We much appreciated the occasions when they drew on their limited funds to support Liberty's advocacy of Christopher's case before the European Court because they recognised that any positive decision by the court could help so many others.

•　　•　　•

We had investigated the arrangements for delivering petitions to 10 Downing Street and obtained approval to do so on 5 September 1998, by which time we had collected 8,525 signatures. We duly turned up with our thick folders of petition forms and were escorted by the duty policeman to the front door of Number 10 where he photographed us delivering the petition. The policeman told us he had been advised to expect us arriving at the head of a delegation from a mass rally in Trafalgar Square. If only we had thought of doing that as well! Signatures to the petition continued to arrive after 5 September and eventually we received just over 10,000.

There were other factors at work: notably the magnificent work of HM Chief Inspector of Prisons, Sir David Ramsbotham, and the continuing stream of reports concerning homicides by those suffering mental illness, of which there were three more cases within a few miles of our rural village. We believe, however, the petition did have some impact in leading the government to decide on some quite positive changes to mental health legislation and to initiate improvements in the provision of mental health care in prisons.

In January 1999 we met the Board of Visitors at Chelmsford Prison who listened carefully to our concerns about what had happened. It had not been easy for me to visit Chelmsford Prison but I had steeled myself to do so as I felt it was a necessary step, not only for myself but also because the Board of Visitors should hear of our experience. One Board member told Paul later at a carol service we attended in the prison that she felt shamed by what we had said. Again we felt encouraged that the Board of Visitors might now see their responsibilities in a new light.

A little later Simon Burns, the Conservative MP for Chelmsford, arranged an adjournment debate on Chelmsford Prison in which he was supported by Alan Hurst, our Labour MP, and Bob Russell, the Liberal Democrat MP for Colchester where Christopher had lived for the last four months of his life. Other positive initiatives we became involved in were attending a House of Lords debate on mentally disordered offenders initiated by the Bishop of Lincoln, the bishop for prisons, and which—most unusually—Paul Boateng the relevant minister at that time came and attended throughout; and participating in a training day on mental health for staff at HM Prison Littlehey, organized by the National Schizophrenia Fellowship.

In addition to concern for the mentally ill there was clearly strong local interest particularly among the churches in how prisoners were treated. Under the auspices of the Justice and Peace Group of the Kelvedon Catholic Church and with the support of all the other local churches, we organized an open public meeting in May 1999 under the title 'The People's Prisoners.' We arrived early at the Kelvedon Institute Hall but found two of the speakers, Alison Gomme, Governor of Chelmsford Prison, and Amanda Westbrook, the mental health manager of the North Essex Health Authority were already there. We appreciated their personal concern for us which led them to give up an evening to speak but we had the impression they were not expecting too many people to attend. In truth nor were we, but we hoped there would be at least 50 so that the evening would not be a total flop. People continued to arrive, more chairs had to be brought out and by the time the meeting was due to start the hall was packed out with more than 120 people.

The other speakers included the deputy head of the Essex Probation Service and a former prisoner. The ex-offender was a mild-looking, inoffensive man, but one who has had a tough life with long stretches of imprisonment. When he said that if 20 years ago he had been asked to 'do for someone' his only response would have been 'for how much?' he had the audience absolutely captured. He was, however, living proof of the potential for even so-called hard criminals to reform with the help of others and he now makes a very positive contribution to the community.

After each of the speakers had made their contribution there was time for questions and comments from the audience and there were many thoughtful and positive contributions. The tone of the meeting was well summed up by Alison Gomme when she said it was the first public meeting she had attended where the evident concern of those present was how to improve the treatment of and position of offenders and not 'to lock them up and throw away the key'. We certainly were greatly encouraged and convinced that there was deep community concern for the welfare of the mentally ill and offenders when the truth was made known. The meeting obviously had a major impact on many of those who attended because even now, years later, we are still meeting people who were there and who tell us how significant the event was for them.

•   •   •

Later in the year, on behalf of the Kelvedon Justice and Peace Group, and with the support of other churches, we applied for a grant from the Health Education Authority to promote the welfare of people with mental illness on World Mental Health Day. There were nearly 500 applications for grants and ours was one of the 48 selected. We had called our proposal 'The Good Samaritan Project' and the funds were used to print and distribute to 7,000 local households a leaflet encouraging the community to offer a welcoming hand and practical support to people suffering mental illness. We were committed to checking the text of the leaflet with the relevant public agencies, which we were pleased to do though we encountered one major disagreement with them. The professionals did not want us to use the word 'suffering' mental illness preferring 'experiencing' mental illness, but we felt it was a denial of the pain involved to pretend it did not involve suffering. I know just how much Christopher suffered and the high incidence of suicide amongst the mentally ill clearly demonstrates their suffering. Moreover the community was more likely to respond with support for those who 'suffered' rather than if they 'experienced' mental illness. So we declined such advice and persisted with our original wording.

These initiatives were effective in enlisting community support but involved considerable effort: booking meeting halls; arranging speakers; promotion of the initiative and press liaison; arranging printing and distribution. After 'The People's Prisoners' meeting we felt we had exhausted the possibility of local initiatives and almost breathed a sigh of relief. Then the Health Education Authority's grant scheme came to our notice. After the circulation of the Good Samaritan leaflet we again felt we had come to the end of what could be done locally. We should have known better!

CHAPTER 23

Success in the European Court

We were told early in 2002 that a decision on our case would be handed down during the year possibly in the first half but cautiously we felt it was more likely to be in the second half. Early in February, Nancy Collins, the lawyer now handling our case for Liberty, checked with the court and was told the decision was not listed. She later went off on three weeks holiday and while she was away we received a message from Liberty that the decision had been taken and would be announced on March 14 by publication on the Internet. The next ten days were an agony of suspense. On the one hand we knew our lawyers were fairly confident and we thought the case would not have been taken on a *pro bono* basis if it was a lost cause; the UK Government's offer of an out of court settlement (*Chapter 20*) had also suggested the they thought our case was stronger than theirs. On the other hand it seemed too much to hope that our cause would finally be vindicated and we had come to recognise that, however just that cause, law and justice do not necessarily coincide.

We did our best to prepare for the decision alerting supportive groups like the Rethinking Crime and Punishment project sponsored by the Esmee Fairbairn Foundation; Sane; the Prison Reform Trust; the Churches Criminal Justice Forum; and the local media. We liaised with Roger Bingham, Liberty's press officer in his campaign to secure national media coverage and also with Gemma Crosland of Oasis Media acting on behalf of the Esmee Fairbairn project.

•   •   •

On March 10 we had to rise at five a.m. so as to be ready to be picked up to be taken to the BBC studio in Colchester to be interviewed on *Today* by Edward Stourton. They only wanted one speaker and Paul urged me to do the three minute interview—and I felt tense and nervous having had little sleep. The segment was recorded and I was informed that it had to be run past their solicitor. Then back home to await a call from Murray Hunt. He rang to say he was receiving the judgement by e-mail and would send a copy immediately.[1] It was good news.

The European Court of Human Rights was satisfied that sufficient information had been known about Richard Linford to demonstrate that there was a real and serious risk to a cellmate. This information had not

---

[1] Application No. 46477/99, *Paul and Audrey Edwards v. The United Kingdom*, 14 March 2002.

been brought to the attention of the prison authorities—as it should have been—and, in addition, the screening examination on arrival at the prison was brief and cursory. There had also been numerous failings in the way Christopher had been treated. These factors combined to establish that there had been a breach of the State's obligation to protect Christopher's life. In considering whether the State had fulfilled its obligation to carry out an effective investigation the court noted that there had been no inquest and the trial had not involved any examination of witnesses. The European Court found that the inquiry was not an effective investigation because it had no power to compel witnesses to attend and had been held in private. We had not been represented and were unable to question witnesses and were not involved to the extent necessary to protect our interests. As a result our right to an effective investigation had been violated. Finally the European Court concluded that the legal processes available to us did not provide an appropriate means of determining our allegation that the authorities failed to protect our son's right to life, nor did we have any possibility of securing any award of compensation for the damage suffered. The European Court commented that we had had to wait until the publication of the final version of the inquiry report to discover the substance of the evidence about what had occurred. It found that given our close and personal concern with the subject matter of the inquiry we could not be regarded as having been involved in the procedure to the extent necessary to safeguard our interests. In our view this judgement applies equally to the failure to make available to us the investigation report which the Metropolitan police submitted to the PCA.

After almost eight years our contentions were completely upheld—and unanimously so by a panel of seven judges. Christopher had been denied his right to life; we had been denied an effective investigation; and denied an effective remedy under the UK legal system. We were overjoyed and quite overwhelmed.

•　　•　　•

The rest of the day was a blur of media activity as television, radio and newspapers contacted us for comments and family and friends rang with congratulations. By the end of the day we were exhausted but uplifted. Justice had been achieved for Christopher, for ourselves and for future mentally ill people and vulnerable prisoners and their families. Nothing could take away the pain and sadness of losing Christopher but now we could offset against it something beneficial to others which had flowed from his tragic death. The reluctance of government agencies to tell us the truth had somehow turned out to be for the good. It had driven us on over every obstacle to the ECHR judgement, the most powerful instrument for necessary change which could have been achieved.

The publicity given to the European Court decision prompted two unexpected contacts. The first was from the magistrate whose children had been confirmed at the same time as Christopher and who had been on the bench when Christopher appeared in court. She stated that she had felt unable to approach us before the European Court decision was handed down. She then gave us her account of what had happened within the magistrates' court complaints system after we had lodged our complaint that the magistrates' concern for Christopher's safety had not been conveyed to the prison. The process had led her, she said, to resign from the bench as it had caused her to lose confidence in the justice system. We were sufficiently concerned by her letter to decide to write to the Lord Chancellor as we believed it was a matter which he, as the Government minister responsible for the judiciary, including the magistracy, should investigate.

The second unexpected contact was a phone call and then a visit by the Spanish tutor who had been in contact with Christopher until shortly before his death. She recalled someone of exceptional intelligence who had readily accepted he would have to go at the pace of the rest of the class and was prepared to help them. He was 'very gentle . . . benefiting from a structure in which to operate' as he did not have the force of personality to impose himself in a group situation. In the last class he attended she had required students to introduce themselves in Spanish to each other in turn so that by repetition they gained command of the language. We agreed with her that this repeated process of introducing himself to strangers in the classroom, as a learning technique, could well have influenced his decision to try and introduce himself to the two young women in Colchester that fateful Sunday afternoon.

As the European Court had ruled we were entitled to an effective investigation into Christopher's death and had not received it, our solicitor wrote to the Home Secretary on 2 May 2002 with our request that an independent public inquiry be set up as soon as possible. Nancy Collins pointed out that the Government's own case to the European Court made reference to a High Court ruling that there was a continuing obligation to investigate a death in custody which occurred prior to the Human Rights Act 1998. She also conveyed our request that we be advised of what steps the Government intended to take in the light of the ECHR judgement. Our request for a new inquiry was supported by our MP, Alan Hurst, who tabled two Parliamentary Questions, by Liberty who issued a press statement, and by the Prisoners' Advice Service. No response had been received by early June so our solicitor pressed again and was told by the Home Secretary's office the delay would be followed up with officials. The fact that three months after the ECHR decision the Home Office had made no response conveyed to us that there was no commitment to accept the ECHR ruling and the message that the family had a right to be involved had fallen on deaf ears.

CHAPTER 24

Restorative Justice

A year or two after Christopher's death we became involved in an ecumenical project called Images of Justice designed to encourage church people to reflect on the implications of the criminal justice system. At one of the meetings we learned for the first time of some practical projects bringing together victims and offenders.

We had been highly critical of the failures of prison officers which led to Christopher's death but I had an overwhelming need to talk to the officers who were the last people to see Christopher alive. I felt if only I could speak to them to understand how it had all happened I might find some sort of peace. I felt also it could be beneficial to them to talk to us: to tell us what had happened might ease the trauma they had experienced. Governor Sinclair had informed us that those officers involved had received counselling; some needed psychiatric help; and some were unable to return to work for months, if at all. Stimulated by this knowledge we approached the Prison Service to suggest a meeting between ourselves and the prison officers who had been involved with Christopher. Alas this request did not lead to the meeting we so much desired. It was not until much later that we found there was a recognised term to cover what we felt—it was called Restorative Justice.[1]

A distinguishing feature of Restorative Justice is that it recognises the status of victims which they are denied by the traditional practices of criminal justice in the UK. Under that practice, victims are regarded as no more than possible witnesses to fact. The hurt they suffer—as we had experienced—is at best dealt with by way of an application for compensation (invariably in their absence) or, at worst, ignored altogether.[2] The second distinguishing feature of Restorative Justice, as its name implies, is that it aims to achieve reconciliation not merely retribution. While affirming that offences merit punishment, it goes further and seeks to bring victim and offender together. It also encourages reconciliation between victim and offender and between offender and society.

It came to me in retrospect that the inquiry could—and should— have been an instrument of reconciliation instead of the divisive

---

[1] For an imaginative modern treatment, see *Restoring Respect for Justice: A Symposium* (1999), Wright M, Winchester: Waterside Press.

[2] In recent times, first the idea of a 'victim impact statement' emerged and then the 'victim personal statement' (see *Practice Direction: Victim Personal Statements*, 16 October 2001 issued by the Lord Chief Justice) whereby the views of the victim are made known to the court. Victims are also now consulted before certain offenders are released from prison.

experience it actually was. Sadly it did not seek from the outset to be a means to achieve mutual understanding between ourselves and the public agencies whose performance was under review.

Early in 2000 the Anglican Diocese of Chelmsford initiated a Restorative Justice Working Group and we were among a number of people invited to the inaugural meeting. We were all feeling our way but agreed to keep going. Then the financial straits of the diocese led to a cutback in staff and the position of the diocesan staff member who had been running the meetings was withdrawn. Suddenly, and quite unasked for, I found myself as the chairperson of the group with Paul bearing most of the administrative responsibility.

We would learn more about Restorative Justice, I was sure, by practising it than by talking about it so the group identified a number of practical initiatives. The first of these was the preparation of a leaflet to be distributed through churches and other faith communities in Essex during Prisoners' Week 2000.[3] We put some effort into designing the leaflet which incorporated quotations from various sources—religious and non-religious—encouraging acceptance of responsibility for prisoners. On the reverse side, under the heading 'Prisoners Are Your Concern', it gave basic facts about the prison population and suggestions of easy and simple ways in which that responsibility could be exercised. It was this same leaflet of which Martin Narey agreed the Prison Service would print 100,000 copies for us (*Chapter 21*). We had perceived the printing of the leaflets by prisoners as in itself an act of Restorative Justice. The Prison Service's support went further, for the Muslim Adviser to the Prison Service had suggested a quotation from the Koran be included alongside quotations from the Old and New Testaments and such diverse lay figures as Oscar Wilde and Nelson Mandela.

The leaflets were duly printed and delivered to our home in about 20 large boxes stamped 'HM Prison Service', which crowded our entrance hall and laundry room for several weeks prior to their distribution. We went through the process of transferring them to over 700 envelopes, most of which were posted to churches, synagogues and mosques while the remainder we delivered to individual churches. Those for the Roman Catholic churches were delivered to a diocesan meeting so that parish representatives could take their copies away.

In Prisons Week 1999, Alison Gomme as prison Governor had supported the holding of an ecumenical service outside Chelmsford Prison on Prison Sunday. This had been a worthwhile but bitterly cold experience. The Restorative Justice Working Group proposed the service be repeated in 2000. This time it was not so cold but drenching rain fell all day, fortunately easing off slightly for most of the service. A number of clergy were there from different churches who had been alerted to the

---

[3] Now known as 'Prisons Week' and hence the variations in the text.

service by the letter accompanying the leaflet. It was encouraging to learn from them and from a number of other contacts with complete strangers how positive the response was to the leaflet and how many people had been encouraged to take a more positive interest in the welfare of prisoners and prisons, including becoming prison visitors or writing letters to prisoners. About 20 people contacted us directly as a result of the leaflet, wishing to become more actively engaged in helping prisoners and ex-prisoners and we were able to put them in contact with appropriate organizations. One building contractor even offered an employment opportunity.

On behalf of the group (whose members include representatives of various denominations; a member of a Board of Visitors; prison chaplains; Essex social services; and individual activists) we had secured a small grant from the Essex Community Foundation which helped pay for some of the activities.

The group agreed to hold two public open meetings to promote understanding of Restorative Justice in the community. The first was held at lunchtime in the YMCA in Romford. There could not have been a more appropriate location, for YMCA staff were playing an active role within Chelmsford Prison trying to help young offenders to establish a new life on release, some of whom occasionally moved into YMCA accommodation. A member of the YMCA staff engaged in this restorative work spoke at the meeting. One of the main speakers demonstrated in his remarks the positive value of Restorative Justice in his own life experience. A young offender himself, he had been supported in prison by the Christian family he had burgled, who took him into their home on his release. This experience of acceptance by his victims led him to become a Christian convert and then a Baptist minister including spending some time as a prison chaplain. He was then a Baptist minister in the Romford area. The other main speaker was the area manager of the Prison Service. He spoke very positively of the new approach to the treatment of offenders which was being introduced into the Prison Service.

We had been responsible for organizing the meeting and promoting it among the churches but the burden was reduced by the local minister taking on board responsibility for promotion in the Romford area. Full responsibility for organizing the second meeting in Chelmsford fell to us. While by now we had gained experience in establishing meeting arrangements and organizing speakers, as well as promotion in the community and the media, no experience takes away the continual worry of whether you have persuaded busy and important people to come and talk to an empty hall.

The speakers at Chelmsford were Angela Phillips the local co-ordinator of Victim Support; Juliet Lyon, the director of the Prison Reform Trust, and the Reverend Dr. Peter Sedgwick, the assistant secretary of the Church of England Board of Social Responsibility and recently appointed chairman of the new ecumenical Churches Forum on Criminal Justice. The speakers promoted—and the audience readily agreed with—a positive reconciling approach towards offenders, arguing that this was in the interest of victims and society as well as the offenders themselves.

Both meetings were well attended and received favourable reactions from those present. The lunchtime meeting in Romford attracted mainly local residents or local practitioners in the criminal justice field such as probation officers, together with some prison officers. The evening meeting in Chelmsford attracted a wider range of participants, including an ex-offender, a prison chaplain, magistrates and a judge as well as those with a personal interest in the issues rather than a professional one.

The success of both meetings confirmed me in my conviction that contrary to the tabloid reaction to offenders—'lock them up and throw away the key'—the majority of the community when provided with the facts will adopt a more positive approach. This conviction has been further strengthened by the experience of talking to various local groups such as Rotary Clubs or Church Prayer Fellowships. Invitations to address these groups followed promotion of the fact that members of the Essex Restorative Justice Working Group were keen to carry their message to small groups. Always the people we have talked to have agreed that society must take a more positive and constructive approach to the treatment of offenders. The Essex Restorative Justice Working Group's recent activities have included encouraging Anglia University, through its chaplaincy, to arrange a public lecture on Restorative Justice by Dr Michael Schluter.[4] Work is in hand to establish an Essex Restorative Justice website.

•　　•　　•

As a result of our experience we are confident of success for the national initiative, Rethinking Crime and Punishment, by the Esmee Fairbairn Foundation under the direction of Rob Allen. The provision of significant funds by this charity to support research and practical work will make more people aware of the inadequacies of the justice system as it now is and of practical ways to change it for the better. I was surprised and delighted to be invited to participate in the national launch of their £2 to 3 million project at the Tower of London in December 2001 and felt nervous as I took my place alongside Jon Snow, Sir Jeremy Isaacs, Baroness Stern and Martin Narey. I gained the confidence to make my

---

[4] Dr Schluter is perhaps best known as the founder and director of the Relationship Foundation in Cambridge. See also the key work relating to that organization with regard to the justice field *Relational Justice; Repairing the Breach* (1994), Burnside J and Baker N (eds.), Winchester: Waterside Press.

contribution from the recognition that the project was acknowledging from the outset that the voice of the victim and that of the family must be heard in the process of reshaping the justice system.

I was, however, quite shocked to hear Martin Narey state that approximately 50 per cent of prisoners are mentally ill. All of the public assurances by those in authority that the lessons of Christopher's tragedy had been learned, and that improvements in the Care in the Community policy, police training, the judicial process and the Prison Service would greatly improve the treatment of mentally disordered offenders had clearly had little impact on the real world situation. Some weeks later the Prison Governors' Association called for government action to stop overcrowding in prisons as the prison population reached 70,000. Why cannot they join with prison doctors and nurses, the Prison Officers' Association and the Police Federation and appeal to the Government to do something about the continued incarceration of mentally ill people?

•   •   •

There are some encouraging signs that attitudes to the criminal justice system are changing: now even the Lord Chief Justice, Lord Bingham, has spoken out against the imprisonment of so many offenders. But not enough leaders of the community are taking an interest in what happens here in the UK. Recently the front pages of the newspapers were full of comments by church leaders, politicians and others in the public eye passing adverse judgement on the way Taliban prisoners were being treated by the US military authorities in Cuba. We noted on an inside page of one Sunday Newspaper a review by a prison doctor of a book about a nineteenth-century prison reformer who had led the way in improving the treatment of mentally disordered offenders detained in Bedlam. The reviewer stated:

> If anyone doubts the reality of madness, or would like a taste of eighteenth century Bedlam before the advent of effective treatments, he could hardly do better than to visit the hospital wing of one of our great prisons. There, what used to be known as lunatics are frequently left to their own devices for months on end. The law forbids them to be treated against their will while they are incarcerated, but there are insufficient beds for them to be treated in hospitals outside. Thus they receive no treatment at all: it is then that the verb 'to rave' comes to have a precise meaning. The contemporary British prison doctor is thus able to empathise with the madhouse-keeper of past centuries, when even partially effective treatments for madness did not exist.[5]

When will the great and the good turn their eyes to the iniquities at home and speak out?

---

[5] Theodore Dalrymple, *Sunday Telegraph*, 20 January 2002

CHAPTER 25

Journey to Hope

Looking back over eight years since Christopher was killed I see that I have consistently been seeking one thing from the outset—the truth. Together with Paul and Clare I wanted to know what happened and why and to have this acknowledged by all involved and on the public record. We have been partially successful because I believe we now know most of the truth of what happened, though I do not know why various people acted in the way they did and certainly not all the truth has been acknowledged.

Reflecting on those years it is hard to believe that we have come such a long way from the depths of despair, anger and frustration to a more sanguine stage. This is due in part to the help and sympathy of so many people whose paths we have crossed during our struggle to obtain some justice for Christopher. There were many times when the exhaustion was so great I felt I could not continue, but my love for Christopher drove me on. I do not believe I failed Christopher during his life and I was resolved that I would not do so after his death.

Our greater equanimity now is also the result of our realisation that in order to have any peace we had to try to turn what was an evil act into a positive message. When I say that the act of Christopher's murder was evil, I in no way suggest that Richard Linford himself was evil. Richard was an extremely ill young man and not responsible for his actions at that time as the trial finding of diminished responsibility shows.

Those early years when we were at the nadir of our despair, when we did not seem to be achieving anything, were indescribable. I think the turning point came with the invitation by Julia Braggins to take a workshop at the ISTD conference in 1997. That invitation gave us for the first time the opportunity to talk to other people involved in and concerned with the injustices in the criminal justice system and from whom we learned a great deal. We learned in particular that within the Prison Service and other organizations there were people who tried to do their very best for prisoners and the mentally ill. We felt encouraged by these encounters to try to increase general awareness of the problems in our own community.

We felt the need for reconciliation with the agencies involved with Christopher's death but this was not always an easy goal to achieve. The Prison Service has since come a long way in recognising a duty of care to prisoners and the need for a more honest and open approach to families. I have every confidence that Martin Narey as Director General is committed to a new and better Prison Service culture. The making of the training video (*Chapter 21*) and the naming of the garden outside Chelmsford Prison after Christopher (*Chapter 21*) were for us very much part of our healing process. I also believe that Chelmsford Prison is now much more part of the local community, due to the interest of the local media in Christopher's tragedy and hopefully to the small contribution we ourselves have made.

Likewise, the NHS trust, after an initial reluctance, acknowledged its failures by naming the intensive care unit 'The Christopher Unit'. It was interesting, we thought, that after consultation with the community, there was no objection to the building of the intensive care unit. This might not have been the case had people not been made aware through the publicity arising from Christopher's tragedy that so many mentally ill people fail to receive the support and service they need.

A sympathetic approach to mentally ill people or to prisoners is not likely to be found in newspaper headlines; yet the injustice of sending mentally ill people to prison, in many cases because they have been failed by Care in the Community, is inexcusable. Many times we have raised the question of why the Government continues to build or support private sector building of more prisons costing billions of pounds, when such a high proportion of prisoners have some level of mental illness and up to five per cent are so seriously mentally ill they, at least, should be in hospital. The answer surely is to build more secure hospitals to accommodate the mentally ill; thus there would not be a need to provide them inappropriately with prison cells. Nobody seems willing to address this fundamental question. Through this book I appeal to the media to take up this issue, media pressure being one of the few prompts to which Government will respond.

•　　•　　•

In March 2001 Paul and I were invited to give a talk at the Annual General Meeting of the Brentwood Diocese Justice and Peace Commission which we entitled *Journey to Hope*. I would like to quote the final part of that talk:

A world in which justice and peace prevailed might be likened to a fine piece of porcelain. Beautiful in itself, an integrated whole of many parts; of perfect quality. But the world in which we live—particularly the world in prison—is not like that. It is fractured; imperfect; unappealing; of poor quality like this broken plate. The broken pieces might represent typical prisoners:

- the teenager, taken into care and abused, who entered into crime to find some status in life;
- the young single mother, taken away from her children because she shoplifted to get something extra for them;
- the mentally ill man, unable to cope in society, denied treatment because he did not ask for it, who committed a minor offence as an expression of his illness;
- the ex-soldier, trained by society to fight, but rejected by society because he did not know anything but fighting after he left the armed services;
- an asylum seeker, knowing neither the language nor the customs of the country, who broke the law without knowing it;
- a man or woman of principle who was imprisoned for demonstrating in support of his/her beliefs; and
- the unknown number who are innocent of any crime and have been wrongly imprisoned.

Most of us looking at these broken pieces would throw them in the bin. But a craftsman, with great patience, care and the right glue, would lovingly put them together again. The plate would be whole once more: damaged but restored.

The work of justice and peace, through Restorative Justice, is surely to restore those broken members of our society in prison to wholeness.

I would add that the work of Restorative Justice (see *Chapter 24*) does not only restore broken members of our society in prison to wholeness but, in our experience, it helps to restore wholeness to victims. It has certainly done that for us.

●   ●   ●

If there is one thing I could change in my lifetime it would be to go back to before 29 November 1994 and ensure that Christopher was properly looked after by the public authorities involved with him. It is an unbearable grief that he had to face such a brutal attack and that I was not able to do anything to help or comfort him in his trauma. I know that cannot be and I can only hope that all we have done since then has ensured that some good has occurred and will continue to occur as a result of his death. He certainly was of the temperament that he would sacrifice himself to help others. His sacrifice has been made and his family have tried and continue to try in justice to him to ensure it has helped others. Good must be made to flow from evil.

Index